D0954338

Reviews from
Industry Experts and Entrepreneurs

I would advise my friends to buy *Stop Working!* and read it. Simple recipe, clear steps, real life examples, everything you need to take the next step in starting and building your own business.

Gerard Paulin, Nike EMEA (Europe, Middle East & Africa) Global Manager.

==========

Mr. Hall has created a standard to which other instructional business guides will be hard pressed to meet. If you aren't doing the things listed in this book, then you're not going to be competitive in today's market.

Alan Jones, MBA, CEO, Rising Sun Group, a technology firm that focuses on large enterprises including J.P. Morgan, Honda and CDW

===========

Stop Working! is a simple, yet profound guide for new business owners who want to succeed without investing a lot of capital or taking on partners. The author explains how you can minimize risks and maximize profits by starting small, growing in measured steps, and using existing business networks to your advantage.

Sammie Justesen, Editor/Entrepreneur (www.doingitwrite.com). Also worked with Mosby, Prentice Hall, and Addison-Wesley

==========

Stop Working! is a clear, concise and easy to understand formula to help you take your business to the next level, without requiring large amounts of capital and resources. All it takes is your idea, commitment and the *Stop Working!* formula and you're on your way to becoming a global player in today's business world.

Keith Buggs, Microsoft Senior Licensing Manager

===========

Never before have I seen such a concise guide on how to build a business by yourself, and how to fulfill your most essential of dreams - security. I love the ability and the hope it gives.

Errol Chung, American Express

==========

This is the book that will make you live the dreams you have been hoping for and earn the "freedom" you rightfully deserve.

Dr. Sydney Sukuta, Ph.D., Physics Professor at San Jose City College. Professor Sukuta has also worked with the University of Phoenix, Coherent, Spectra-Physics, and JDS Uniphase in Silicon Valley California.

===========

The book is very strong at projecting the common mistakes of a first time business owner and solutions to correct them. The author did an excellent job of keeping it interesting and educational from the beginning to the end.

Sanjay Kumar, Technology Consultant. He has worked with Honda, Qualcomm, and Covance.

===========

If a journey of a thousand miles begins with a single step, and your journey is in business, make *Stop Working!* your first step! *Stop Working!* outlines all the essential components of starting your own business, or improving one that you have already started. It demystifies many of the trends and forces of the contemporary, global business environment so that anyone, from a high school student to an M.B A., can not only understand, but can apply TODAY to get results.

Dan Fink, Global Supply Chain Consultant. He has worked with PeopleSoft, NEC/Packard Bell, Verizon, Fairchild Semiconductor, and Harcourt Publishing

STOP

Working!

Start a business, globalize it, and generate enough cash flow to get out of the rat race!

By Rohan Hall

This book contains the ideas and opinions of its author and is designed to provide reliable, competent and accurate information on the subject matter covered. It is sold with the understanding that the author and publisher are not engaged in rendering legal, accounting, financial or other professional services by publishing this book. To address each individual's situation, the appropriate professional should be consulted regarding suggestions made in this book or inferences made from it. The publisher and author specifically disclaim all responsibility for any risk, loss, or liability incurred directly or indirectly as a consequence of the use or application of the content of this book.

Copyright @ 2004 by Rohan Hall
Published by Eye Contact Media, Inc.
Printed in the United States of America.

All rights reserved.
No part of this book may be reproduced or transmitted in any form or by any means, electronic or mechanical, including photocopying, or by any information storage and retrieval system without permission in writing from the publisher, with the exception of short excerpts for book reviews.

For information, contact:
Eye Contact Media, Inc.
www.eyecontactmedia.com
info@eyecontactmedia.com

All trademarks and copyrights mentioned in this book are the properties of their respective owners.

ISBN 0-9729187-3-6

Printed in the USA
10   9   8   7   6

Stop Working!

Dedicated

To my parents, because everything starts at home
To my wife because every time I look into your eyes I see a
beautiful future.
To my brothers and my sister because you are always my
inspiration
To my nieces and nephews, you are the future

To happiness – may everyone find it!

Rohan Hall

Contents

Rohan Hall

Stop Working!

Introduction

What does it take to build a successful business to the point that you can actually stop working?

===================

Less than a year after I started my new company it became a global player. Our customers come from all over the United States, Europe, Japan, Asia, Australia, South America, and Africa. Sales are going great, with increased growth every month – and best of all, I spend only a few minutes per day managing the company. Even more shocking to many is the fact that I have no employees.

This is the age of globalization, technology, and integration. By learning how to utilize these three influences you can build a business with very little capital that will compete with multinational organizations.

Stop Working! is different than other wealth-related books because it isn't a motivational text. Instead, it shows you how to build a profitable business from a small investment; a business that will yield unlimited cash flow. *Stop Working!* also teaches you how to expand your business by aligning with global partners.

Many "get rich" books come across like cheerleaders, pumping you full of vague ideas and goals. Or they give you one piece of the puzzle, but fail to provide the information you need to start, build and grow a profitable business. *Stop Working!* gives you all the pieces you will need to build your business and get rich.

But starting a business is only the first step in becoming wealthy. As a business owner you'll also need to build products, build or use distribution channels, create strategic relationships, and form an effective marketing and advertising campaign. How are these things done? How long will it take to become profitable? What does it take to become wealthy? When can **you** stop working?

Stop Working! goes beyond the typical "how to start a business" formulas. I provide real life examples of global organizations I've work with, describing what I did to help these companies maintain their profitability and market positions. These companies include various fortune 500 companies, as well as my own organizations. You learn how to take advantage of globalization, instead of being a victim of it. My goal is to show you <u>exactly</u> how to build a company from the bottom up, and then how to use that company to create unlimited cash flow so you can finally stop working and get out of the rat race.

Stop Working!

Rohan Hall

Section I

Globalization – Your Path to Wealth

Rohan Hall

Chapter 1

Job Security

———————

I would have preferred to make my money the old fashion way – to inherit it! However, I wasn't that fortunate, and I suspect you weren't either.

I immigrated to the United States with my family when I was only 13 years old. We were never wealthy and my parents worked hard every day just to make ends meet. I watched my parents work very hard, pursuing the American Dream. They are people of the highest values, similar to many immigrants who came before us, and those who arrived since. One thing I learned from my parents was the possibility of having my own business. The promise of financial and personal freedom was always our dream. We were independent thinkers and thought the American Dream could be found by owning a business.

Even with their own business, my parents worked long hours to make a living. I grew up watching them work hard, but never become wealthy. They made enough money to take care of the basic needs, but not enough to be considered wealthy. Although they enjoyed the freedom and satisfaction of owning their own business, the promise of wealth and retirement seemed to elude them. Bank loans became bank debts, and a hard economic turn almost wiped them out.

Watching them struggle, I wondered why some people succeeded in business, while others struggled all their lives and never became wealthy.

I won't try to convince you to start your own business. You're reading this book because you've already made that decision. For me, owning a business is a part of my life. I started my first enterprise at the age of 19 and have had many other businesses since then. But don't be fooled. In addition to being a business owner, I've also spent years in the corporate world, working my tail off, hoping to get recognized or promoted. I did well for awhile and was filled with high hopes and aspirations. I wanted to climb the ladder all the way to the top.

When I started my first business, I did so because I thought it was cool and I shared my parents' dreams. I was a 19-year-old college student in 1984 when something new came on the market – the Personal Computer. As a computer student, I thought it would be cool to build these Personal Computers from scratch and sell them. I was working two jobs at the time and enrolled full time in the local community college. I was also VP of the computer club on campus. Where did I have the time to start a business? I really don't know. I just felt the need to do it. So I did.

I didn't become Michael Dell from this. In fact, I didn't even make enough money to quit my other jobs. When my grades were affected and the income wasn't rushing in, I quietly discontinued the business. It was my first endeavor and I'm still proud when I think about it. The business was profitable, but not sustainable. I did the entire thing from my little $280/month apartment. After that I decided to pursue a corporate career as a computer programmer, because I just loved the fact that people were willing to pay me to do something I enjoyed. Plus, I really needed the money.

I'm proud of my first business when I look back, because it shows I had a vision when I was only a teenager. I had a vision of the future, and I was right. I also had the technical skills to pull it off, but I lacked the business skills to make this venture successful.

Now I'm much older and significantly more experienced. I just watched a great meltdown of visionaries – often called the Internet bust. I watched many young, intelligent visionaries start their own businesses to pursue a dream. They weren't successful, but I'm convinced they were correct in their vision of the future. Unfortunately, being right about the future of a business idea doesn't create a successful venture.

So what does it take to create a successful business? What did Bill Gates, Michael Dell, Russell Simmons, Sean Combs and the many other successful business people know or *do* that makes them different from those who failed? What did Michael Dell know about building a computer business that I didn't know?

Actually, he knew a lot. There's a phrase you will come to respect in this book: *strategic partnerships*. Another important term is *business processes*. These two concepts are at the core of every successful business, yet most people are unfamiliar with their true meaning in everyday business. When people talk about business they think of negotiating, selling, deal-making etc. These are all good things, but they're only a small part of the big picture.

The Job Security Lie

I continued my college education while working two jobs. Eventually, I found a "secure" job as a computer programmer that paid a good salary. This was nice – only one job to go to.

I worked hard and had high aspirations for climbing the corporate ladder. In our early twenties, it's easy to get swept away with the promise of the good life and corporate success. I always had a knack for technology. I considered myself a whiz kid and believed there was no code I couldn't write. I begged for new projects and read every technology book I could find. I remember accepting my first database project; a database called Image on a system made by Hewlett Packard. The system was called HP3000 and it was the high tech of the day. The two instruction manuals contained hundreds of pages of material to learn. I took the Image database manuals and the Basic programming language manuals home with me and spent the night reading. The next day I started working on my first corporate database-programming project.

For the next ten years I worked for various companies trying to find a way to the top. I was deep in the trenches as a programmer, analyst, and project manager. In my 10th year, I simply gave up. I just couldn't lie to myself anymore. The starry-eyed kid had become the disillusioned adult. In that ten year period I'd been fired, laid off, and quit several jobs. Maybe the corporate thing just wasn't for me. Or maybe I saw things I couldn't forget or ignore. The reality was, I finally understood how companies worked – from the inside out. I knew exactly how companies operated and exactly why job security could only be a fantasy.

During those years I saw CEOs, senior VPs, managers, and other employees get fired, laid off, or simply died emotionally. There were times that everyone I knew seem to be looking for a new job. No one was happy and everyone lived in fear of losing his or her job or falling out of favor with the boss.

I worked for a company when I was still in my 20s that got rid of three CEOs in two years. Each time a new CEO came on board he'd replace all the senior VPs with his/her own people. Each time this happened, the "beating" trickled down the entire corporate chain. Over the two and a half-year period I was with that company 40% of the staff was let go.

I survived the staff reduction, but I wasn't the lucky one. I inherited the work of three people, with no extra pay. But I was happy to still have a job, so I never complained. People were actually afraid to talk to each other, because anything they said might be used against them "the next time." No one trusted anyone and everyone was afraid to make a mistake. The stress was so great that one day I woke up with my pillow covered with blood from a severe nosebleed. Terrified, I went to see the doctor.

"Stress," he said. I just didn't know stress could do this to you. The doctor suggested I make some changes in my life, and shortly after that I left the company.

Those years still haunt me. What was I working toward if even VPs and CEOs can get fired? What type of retirement could I have if I didn't believe the company would be there for me in my later years? I'd seen people let go after working 15 or more years for the company. It wasn't their fault. They'd worked hard every day, building the company. Was there no loyalty? The sad truth is: "No, there is none."

During those years I constantly worried about keeping my job. That was bad enough, but what affected me the most were older people who had families to support. I was still young and without responsibilities, but others around me struggled because of their age and responsibilities. What would they do? Was this not their secure job? Was this not an investment in their future, their retirement plan? If a CEO's position isn't safe, then how can any position be safe? Was the promise of job security just a lie?

Today
Years later, we see that things aren't any better. The new millennium started with the fall of Enron. Thousands of hard-working employees woke up and learned the sad truth I learned years before: There is no job security when you work for someone else. The reason is very simple – *you have no control over the decisions the company makes.*

Since the beginning of the new millennium, major layoffs, corporate mistrust, and Wall Street corruption are so common that we're surprised when we don't see bad news in the newspaper or news reports.

As I write this, PeopleSoft acquired J.D. Edwards. Layoffs are planned from this merger. Other companies such as Sun Microsystems, 3Com, Boeing, HP, Agilent, and American Airlines have announced layoff plans over the past few months. Oracle is in the process of a hostile takeover of PeopleSoft. What do you think will happen to the employees in both companies if this hostile takeover happens? Don't be surprised if many are downsized straight out the door. Comcast Cable Company has tried to do a hostile takeover of Disney. Cingular has bought AT&T Wireless. You know what will happen – more layoffs will probably follow. In fact, if you read this book ten years from now, you'll see that things haven't changed much. The only thing that will change is the name of the company doing the layoffs, the reason for the layoffs, and names of the people whose lives are shattered.

This is not a negative prediction. It's simply the life cycle of business. As companies grow, they acquire other companies in order to maintain a competitive edge in their market, or to expand into other markets. Each merger or acquisition brings duplication of human resources. In other words, each company will end up with excess employees performing the same jobs. It makes no sense for companies to keep both sets of employees. So they make the business decision to consolidate these functions. Your job may be secure for the moment, but someone else has to go.

Stop Working!

Besides mergers and acquisitions, we see corporate rightsizing or downsizing. This simply means a company decides it can save money by reducing expenses or long term liability. One of the primary reductions companies make to save money is the "head count," AKA employees. So there you are, working hard every day, planning on sending your kids to college or having that great vacation. The executives determine they need a cost reduction and they use various ways to determine who should go. You just happen to be one of those selected. What about the security you felt you had? It was just an illusion.

And even without mergers, acquisitions and consolidations, companies will always seek ways to increase efficiency and profits. In other words, they'll find ways to increase profitability via technology and improved business processes. In many of these cases, increased efficiency often means reduced staffing needs.

I'm constantly amazed when people ask if I'm concerned about not having security because I work for myself. Or they'll ask when I'll decide to get a real job and work for someone. I hold my tongue because I realize they don't understand how companies work. They don't realize that a company's primary goal is to be profitable for the owners or shareholders, and that employees are a necessary liability for companies. To remain competitive and increase profitability for owners and shareholders, companies will *always* strive to find ways to reduce their liabilities and increase revenue. The hard truth is that employees are an expensive long-term liability, and if a company can reduce this liability to increase profits, it won't hesitate to do so.

The lesson I learned years ago remains true today: if *you don't control the company, you don't control your future*.

Why you work for someone else

People have jobs for a practical reason: They receive a paycheck every two weeks for showing up. The big challenge is to avoid being fired – something they have some control over – or avoid getting laid off, over which they have little or no control.

People also have jobs because they really believe this means financial security. They believe if they work hard and long enough it's possible to climb the corporate ladder and make enough money to live the good life. They also hope they'll save enough money for retirement, or the company will help them when they retire. Some even believe Social Security will be there in abundance waiting for them.

But mostly, people have jobs because they find starting their own business is risky and a lot of work. Actually, this is correct. Most new companies fail within the first year, and only a small percentage actually succeed. The point is not to focus on the failures, but to consider the successful companies. How did the owners do it? What does it really take to build a successful business?

You Aren't Alone

As an entrepreneur, you've probably asked yourself, *"What does it take to become successful in business?"* You aren't alone.

Babson College in the United States and London Business School in the United Kingdom, with sponsorship from the Ewing Marion Kauffman Foundation in the United States have spearheaded a research program to study entrepreneurial activities globally.

This Herculean effort of scholars from all over the world includes prestigious business schools and universities in both developed and developing countries. Their ongoing quest is to understand how entrepreneurship impact national economies, how countries are different in entrepreneurship, and to understand what social and economic conditions contributes to entrepreneurs' success in business. The goal is the support, sponsorship, and education of entrepreneurs and students towards the advancement of entrepreneurship globally.

Stop Working!

A result of this research is the Global Entrepreneurship Monitor (GEM) report.

The 2003 Global Entrepreneurship Monitor report included 41 countries and concludes a variety of fascinating information that every entrepreneur should be aware of. According to the GEM

About 300 million are involved in trying to start almost 200 million new firms.

The total population of the United States is 290 million people. You therefore have more people in the 41 GEM countries trying to start businesses than there are people in the entire population of the United States.

Entrepreneurship is truly a global phenomenon; it isn't just the American Dream, it's a worldwide dream. Individuals like yourself all over the globe are asking similar questions and are pursuing the same goals of financial and personal independence.

Educational attainment and relative household income affect the motivations for entrepreneurship more than the actual level of participation. Those with more education and from households with higher income are more likely to pursue opportunity entrepreneurship. Those with less education and from poor households are more likely to pursue entrepreneurship out of necessity. The personal context has a major impact on the pursuit of entrepreneurship; those that know other entrepreneurs, see good opportunities for starting a business, and think they know how to start a business are 10 times more likely to be active than those that do not have positive responses to these three items.[1]

---

[1] Reynolds, P.D., W.D. Bygrave, and Autio E. 2004. Global Entrepreneurship Monitor: 2003 Executive Report. Babson College, London Business School, and the Kauffman Foundation, page 77, 88

Why Businesses Fail

There's only one way a company can be profitable: Revenue must exceed expenses. I don't need to tell you this, because it's common sense. It doesn't take an MBA to understand this simple fact, and you certainly don't need 20 years of business experience to get it. But in that case, why do so many companies ignore this fact? Why did the entire dotcom sector ignore profitability for the hope of market shares? Because it's easier to talk about profitability than to achieve it.

Here are three of the top reasons companies fail:
- High overhead
  - You can't afford employees
  - You can't afford expensive equipment
  - You can't afford to do it by yourself
- Low revenue
  - You need your product to become global
  - Your product should be sold in multiple markets
  - You need partners that legitimize you
- Poor business skills
  - You need to understand the money
  - You need to understand business processes
  - You need to embrace technology
  - You need to understand and embrace the global economy
  - You need to focus on your core competence

High Overhead

When you start a business that's buried under debt, you've created an enormous obstacle for yourself. I know the current thought process of having huge loans or investors to start a business, but I'm fundamentally against it – especially if it is your first business. If you're an experienced business owner then you'll know how to leverage that debt in your favor. However, most people who haven't *owned* a successful business are likely to fall into a debt-ridden trap. This includes people who've been executives in other businesses. Managing a division of a Fortune 500 company isn't the same as owning your own enterprise. The risk and reward factors are significantly different. The best guideline is: If you've never owned a successful business, then stay as far away from debt as possible.

You really can't afford to hire employees for your small business at first. Employees create a big expense. If you pay an employee $10 per hour for a 40-hour week, you've spent $400 for that week. What happens if you only made $100 during that time? Multiply that by four employees for the same week. Even if you multiply your revenue by four, your cost will be $1,600. In your first week in business you'll lose $1,200 from that one expense. And that's assuming that you actually make any revenue in the first few weeks or months, which many businesses do not.

Week One				
	Employee 1	Employee 2	Employee 3	Employee 4
Hours	40	40	40	40
Rate	10	10	10	10
	$400	$400	$400	$400
Total Revenue	$400			
Total Wages Paid	$1,600			
Net Revenue/(Loss)	($1,200)			

One of the big differences between having your own business and working for a corporation is that corporations try to justify budgets by having high expenses. Sometime that's through the number of employees, the amount of equipment, or the type of projects they undertake. As a small business owner you can't afford to think that way. Every dollar you spend must be thought of as a percentage of revenue leaving your pockets. If that expense becomes greater than the potential revenue, then you must think carefully about spending the money.

You can't afford expensive equipment. Most people think they should have the best equipment when starting a new business. I disagree. I think you need *access* to the best equipment, but you don't need to buy or lease it. The cost of the expensive equipment can sink you into debt immediately. You'll spend years making payments on it. Even though you can depreciate the value of the equipment and get some tax write offs, you still have that expense every month.

You can't afford to do it by yourself. Well if you don't have employees and you don't have equipment, then how can you run a business? How can you manufacture your products and operate your business? To build and run your business you should build strategic relationships with others who already have skilled employees, an investment in technology and state of the art equipment, and solid business processes. Your relationship with these people will alleviate your need for high overhead.

Your expense should always be calculated as a percentage of your revenue. It's impossible to have a business without incurring expenses. However, a change of paradigm you should take advantage of is happening in the market. This involves thinking of expenses as a percentage of revenue instead of an overhead cost. When you think of expenses as an overhead cost, you often don't see the full impact on your business and the bottom line. You just accept certain monthly costs as part of your business – including employees and the cost of purchasing or leasing expensive equipment. We generally refer to this as fixed cost, or overhead. The new paradigm regarding expense is to make all expense a variable cost. That is, each dollar you spend on your company should be linked back to the way it directly affects profit.

Stop Working!

By creating strategic relationships with other companies, you have the opportunity to negotiate the cost of their services. In some cases there will be a monthly flat fee; a fixed cost for their services. For example, to take customer orders for your company for one month, your strategic partner might charge a fixed cost of $400. I don't like those types of agreements because I may have only 12 sales orders, or I might have 200 orders. It would be a good investment if 200 customers ordered my product, but a bad deal if I only had 12 orders. Either way, I would have a $400 bill each month – even if no orders were received.

Monthly Fixed Cost $400

	Orders	Cost per order
January (Good deal)	200	$2.00
February (Bad deal)	12	$33.33
March (Very Bad deal)	0	$400
April (Very Good deal)	850	$.47

Instead, I strive to have a per-unit cost and calculate that per unit cost as a percentage of gross sales. A unit in this case would be an order. Therefore if I have a per-unit cost of $1 per order, I pay $12 for 12 orders, or $200 for 200 orders.

Per Unit Cost of $1 per Order

	Orders	Cost per order	Total Cost
January (Good deal)	200	$1.00	$200.00
February (Good deal)	12	$1.00	$12.00
March (Good deal)	0	$1.00	$0
April (Good deal)	850	$1.00	$850

My cost per order always remains the same. As my sales increase or decrease, so do my costs. Therefore, each cost is always directly linked to profitability. In the example below, my expense is always 4% of my Gross Sales. My Net Sale is therefore always 96% of my Gross Sales, regardless of the

19

number of orders for that month. When there are no sales, I have no expenses.

Retail Sale per item = $25

	Orders	Cost per order	Total Cost	Gross Sales	Net Sales	Expense % of Sales
January Sales	200	$1.00	$200.00	$5,000	$4,800	4.00%
February Sales	12	$1.00	$12.00	$300	$288	4.00%
March Sales	0	$1.00	$0	$0	$0	0%
April Sales	850	$1.00	$850.00	$21,250	$20,400	4.00%

This same concept can be applied to cost per order handling, cost per product manufactured, cost per products shipped, etc. The main point here is that my costs can be directly tied to a transaction. If my transactions per month increase, so do my expenses – and my revenue. My expenses can therefore be calculated as percentage of revenue. This is also true in reverse. If transactions fall, my revenue falls and my expenses drop in proportion. When I do my expenses I don't ever have to worry if I'm profitable, since the total of all my expenses will be a percentage of the total revenue. This direct correlation of expense to revenue always helps me keep a positive bottom line of profitability.

Low Revenue
You need your product to become global. The world has changed. Globalization is one of the biggest opportunities for today's business owners. In the future, it will become more and more impractical for companies to maintain a strong market position without a global strategy. Operating only in the local market will significantly reduce your revenue potential. Products that are needed in your city are needed in the national market as

well as in other countries. Your revenues could multiply significantly by introducing your product to a global market.

Your product should be sold in multiple markets. Your products can be sold in various markets, including geographic, ethnic and cultural venues. Once your product is inserted into the global market you may need to make changes for different markets. Such changes might include language for books and music; units of measurement for certain equipment; regional specifications, etc. You only need to build the product once, modify or retool the product, then resell it into different markets as desired.

You need partners that legitimize you. Strategic partners not only introduce you to new markets, they also make you immediately legitimate and credible to their network. Customers may be considerably more comfortable buying your product from your established strategic partner than buying directly from your new company. Use these established relationships in your favor. A classic example of this is Microsoft's relationship with IBM in the early 80s. No one knew who Microsoft was back then, but everyone was comfortable using their products because of their relationship with IBM. IBM was a household name and people said, *you can't go wrong if you buy IBM.* The little startup by Bill Gates was immediately legitimate and global because of their strategic partnership with IBM.

Poor Business Skills
You need to understand the money. Sometimes we like to pass the financial responsibility of our business to an accountant. We often believe that if we focus on sales and forget the money, everything else will be Okay. That isn't true. Sales are only a single component of the business infrastructure. You don't have to be an accountant or understand complex accounting, but you *do* need to understand the financial impact of each decision you make. For example, it's irresponsible to increase expenses in the

hope of getting more sales without understanding the impact of your actions on the bottom line. Your accountant can tell you what you did – after it's too late. If you arm yourself with basic financial information it could make the difference between a profitable company and a financial failure.

You need to understand business processes. This is another area business owners and executives try to avoid. The focus is often on increasing sales, which is good. You always want to increase sales. However, by increasing the efficiency of your business processes you can increase sales *and* reduce expenses. You get double benefits each time you find a way to make your company operate more efficiently.

You need to embrace technology. Managers and business owners who fear or resist technology always place themselves at a disadvantage. Technology is at the heart of efficiency, integration, and innovation. The correct application of technology can save your organization tons of money every year. Technology is the big integrator. The flow of data through your organization should be like the flow of blood through your body. It should be effortless. Your various processes should be integrated and require minimum intervention from you.

You need to understand and embrace the global economy. The global economy is here – and it's here to stay. Your competitors are already using this global economy to become more competitive, more efficient and richer. Competitors who focused on local business in their country years ago are now taking customers from your own back yard. To compete and survive in this new millennium you'll have to make globalization a core part of your business strategy. To ignore this is to cap your growth and open your back door to the competition.

You need to focus on your core competence. There's too much work to be done and you can't do everything yourself. Large

Stop Working!

organizations struggle to keep up with the pace of today's changing markets. Small business trying to do it by themselves will not be able to compete. You need partners with influence, access, and resources. By choosing the right partners you can stay ahead of the curve while focusing on your core competence. As a business owner, your core competence is to provide the strategic vision for your organization, structure the relationships that will help you carry out the vision, and create new innovative products to put into the marketplace.

Rohan Hall

Chapter 2

Strategic Business Entities

Business structures are going through an evolution that began in the early nineties with technology that focused on integration. One of these innovations is called client/server technology – a process that focuses on connecting disparate (dissimilar) technologies within an organization.

Client/server technologies evolved to what we generically call Internet technology. This took integration to another level. Internet or web based technology facilitated the integration of corporations, along with their partners, suppliers and customers.

This emergence of new technology spawned a variety of applications to optimize the way we do business – not just within an organization, but through an entire network of dissimilar businesses and technology.

Companies have invested billions of dollars since the 90s to make their organizations more strategically competitive in the new global market. It's a race to see who will be ready to compete in the millennium. Various technologies will help meet this goal: ERP – Enterprise Resource Planning, CRM – Customer Resource Management, SCM – Supply Chain Management, SFM – Sales Force Management, and EAI – Enterprise Application Integration are a few enterprise scale technologies that help organizations gain a competitive edge.

Armed with technology and newly optimized business processes, corporations are expanding via mergers and acquisitions. Large organizations become Mega Organizations and national companies go global.

So how can a small business survive and thrive in this new era of global competitiveness? By changing the game and by changing the rules.

Infrastructure of a Mega Organization

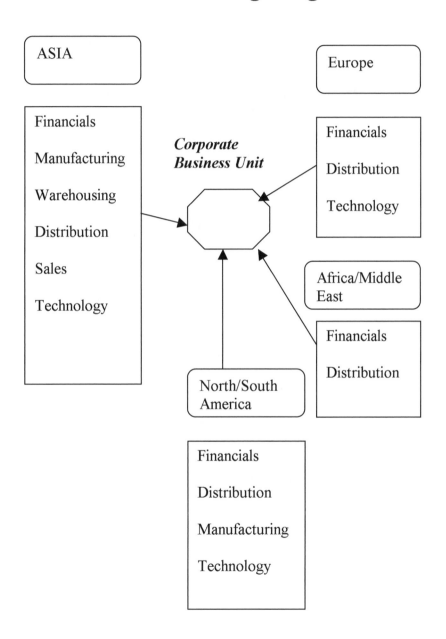

The strength of a Mega Organization lies in its resources. These companies can afford to hire the best and the brightest, and they invest millions of dollars in cutting edge technology. Over the last 15 years they've re-engineered their organization to use the best of breed technology and business processes, leading to global integration of their businesses.

These organizations span the globe in one way or another. They're represented in most major countries and spend huge sums of money investing in emerging countries.

Mega Organizations rely on integrated business processes inside their organization, as well as integration with partners, suppliers and customers. They outsource tasks that aren't strategic to their growth, such as check processing, customer call centers, manufacturing, and distribution. They focus on vital issues such as strategic planning, product development, emerging markets, and globalization.

However, Mega Organizations do have weaknesses. Their greatest strength is long term strategic planning and cash flow, but they often can't react quickly to market opportunities. They aren't the slow, antiquated machines they once were, but they aren't agile enough to react immediately to new market changes.

As a small to midsize business owner, you can use this to your advantage. You shouldn't copy the business model use by Mega Organization, because it's too expensive and you cannot afford it. Change your business model and you can change the game. You'll be able to compete on a level playing field with Mega Organizations, *on your own terms*. To do this, you need to create an Agile Organization.

Stop Working!

Infrastructure of an Agile Organization

Your Company

Strategic Vision
Relationship Management
Product Design

↓

Strategic Partnerships

ASIA – EUROPE – NORTH AMERICA – AFRICA –
AUSTRALIA – MIDDLE EAST- SOUTH AMERICA

Financials

Manufacturing

Warehousing

Distribution

Sales

Technology

Marketing

Fulfillment

Why you can compete with and beat a Mega Organization
You can out-compete a Mega Organization because of
your strategic partnerships. In fact, some of your strategic
partners will be Mega Organizations as well.

When Microsoft provided DOS for IBM in the early 80s,
they were partnering with a Mega Organization. This partnership
gave Microsoft as much market access as IBM's products.
Microsoft was, in essence, a combination of IBM and Microsoft.
Companies that bought MS DOS were in fact buying the
equivalent of an IBM product. By using IBM's distribution
channel, Microsoft was also using IBM's global network of
partners that were involved in the distribution of that product.
Microsoft's cost in this relationship was most likely a discount of
their retail price. For example, if DOS cost $50 retail, then IBM
may have paid Microsoft $25 (a 50% discount). Microsoft then
created similar strategic relationships with other technology
vendors, using these relationships to dominate the business and
technology world.

New technological advances have made such
relationships easier today that ever before in history. You merely
need to surf the Internet to find potential business partners
waiting for the opportunity to do business with you.

With this new business structure you can have immediate
global access instead of spending years building it. Imagine
having a distribution agreement with IBM, HP, Intel, Microsoft,
or a similar business in your field? By using their distribution
channel you'll achieve immediate global access without the cost
of building the distribution channel yourself. Your cost of using
their distribution channel will typically be in the form of some
discount or fee based on the products sold through that channel.
Since the fee will be a percentage of gross or net sales, you will
be profitable while selling your product in the new global
economy.

You can also beat your competing Mega Organization,
because you have the same access, but not the same cost. The
size of your business allows you to shift with the changing

economy – something that's difficult for your Mega Organization competitor.

But what does it take to build such an Agile Organization? Does it take years? Is it expensive? Who do you need to know?

Strategic Business Processes for An Agile Business Entity

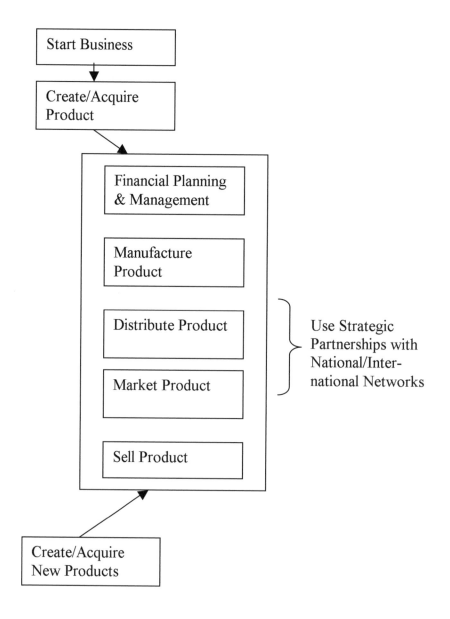

Enterprise Integration

Enterprise resource planning (ERP) is a process that involves combining (integrating) best of breed technologies and business processes. The very essence of ERP is to automate and integrate routine business processes throughout an organization.

To survive and stay ahead of the competition, global enterprises have spent billions on acquiring and implementing ERP technologies over the last decade. As companies expand their product lines and move into new territories, they need more streamlined ways to manage their businesses.

As an ERP consultant I've helped optimize a variety of global organizations using technologies from PeopleSoft, SAP, and Oracle. My primary area of expertise is PeopleSoft.

I've also trained some of the top consulting firms and implementation partners on ERP technology. This includes various *Big 6* consulting firms, PeopleSoft employees, and Global 1000 corporations. I've done this throughout the USA, Europe and Asia.

In the first chapter I told you I worked in corporate America for years, and finally became disillusioned with the entire corporate structure. Once I understood the details of how corporations work, it was crystal clear that companies simply couldn't afford to give me the long-term security or financial growth I needed. If they did so for every employee, they wouldn't be competitive and they'd go out of business.

I eventually walked away from my employee status and started another business; a consulting firm. Our core competence is integrating business processes for Fortune 500 and Global 500 corporations with technology. These companies use our services to help them become more competitive in local and global markets.

The primary goal of this work is to go into a company (usually a multi billion dollar Mega Organization), identify, and optimize every business process used by the company. This means we identify every paper and process, every type of phone call and order, how products are received and orders are shipped, how cash is received, and how products are manufactured. At the end of the analysis stage of a project we know every detail about each business process in the area of the company we're reviewing and how it ties to the company's strategic direction.

We also analyze every technology the company uses. What happens when someone takes an order with one computer software versus another? How does data flow from one technology to another? How does data flow between subsidiary business entities versus the corporate entities? How does data flow to and from external partner organizations? What types of computer software and hardware are being used? How many transactions are processed daily, weekly, and monthly for each business process? How does data map to different technologies, departments, and business entities? What kind of reporting is currently being done, is it accurate, does it meet corporate directives or local regulatory requirements?

The level of details required to be successful with these projects is enormous. We use various methodologies to manage this flow of vital information. When we finish identifying how the organization is interconnected and exactly how they do business on a detailed level, then we determine how to improve their way of doing business. In other words, if it takes eight steps to take and record a customer's order, how could we improve this? Is it possible to reduce these eight steps to three, two, or even one step? Could we actually eliminate some processes all together? What does this process improvement mean for the company? If we go from eight steps to two steps, are we talking about an improvement of 400% in this one business function? What would it take to improve a global organization's efficiency by 400%? How much money will they save? How much more competitive will they become?

Our primary goal is helping companies operate more efficiently. Efficiency translates directly to profits.

ERP technology was created specifically for this task. Companies that used four or five disparate applications move to a single integrated technology. Technologies that couldn't communicate with each other are seamlessly integrated and efficient. The data flows through the organization seamlessly empowering the organization to make better decisions and become more competitive in their particular markets.

In major companies, before this type of integration, it was common to see several generations of technologies that didn't work with each other. In one company, for instance, you might find four or five different types of order taking software located on different computer operating systems. Companies lost the competitive edge because they couldn't see the full picture of their inventory and how that tied into manufacturing and cash flow.

By integrating the entire organization companies, become more competitive. Orders in Japan and France are immediately reflected in the corporate office in New York. Low inventory quantities in Sweden can trigger new manufacturing orders in Malaysia, which triggers purchasing orders in the USA.

This process is a part of what's called Globalization – integrating business processes internationally. It includes becoming local in language, currency, and local regulations, while remaining global in processes, practices and technology.

The cost for the projects and technologies I just mentioned are in the millions of dollars. A company will spend $10 million to $50 million or more on a project of this magnitude. When they're finished, they know they'll be competitive for years to come.

The downside of this is, of course, that people lose their jobs because as the company becomes more efficient they require fewer employees to do the work that the technology now does

The Bottom Line
Large companies are successful when they have appealing products, a cost efficient way to manufacture these products, a distribution network to easily get these products from their manufacturing plants to the warehouses and customers, plus a global market to sell these products. Additionally, they have the

technology and business processes required to efficiently manage the business.

A company can downsize without worrying about the loss of employees because they rely on technology more than human resources. For example, when the order-taking process is streamlined and well established, it's easy to replace and train employees as needed – or hire seasonal employees from a temp agency. The more standardized the technology and business process, the easier it is to replace people. With this kind of integrated technology, the workers are less relevant as long as the business processes are standardizes through technology.

Because of this, technologies that integrate business practices, such as Enterprise Resource Planning (ERP), Supply Chain Management (SCM), Customer Relationship Management (CRM), and Financial Management software have dominated the market over the last two decades. These technologies cost a company millions of dollars, but they create a more integrated and competitive organization with a need for less human resources. The end result is a stronger bottom line over time.

I've been involved in projects where entire business units were laid off, warehouses closed, and entire departments were let go. Where it may have taken 20 people to run and operate an IT (information technology) department for instance, you may now need only two or three. For companies, this means more profits and less cost – a stronger bottom line.

Why you need to understand this

As a small or mid-size business owner, you need to understand how large organizations work, because they are your competitors. Think of all the small businesses you knew of while growing up. Where are they now? Most have been replaced by retail chains, malls, and multinational businesses. This trend will not end. A small shop isn't really competing with the other small shop across the street. It's competing with Wal-Mart, Target, Barnes & Noble, and other Mega organizations and large department stores. The other small shop across the street is simply trying to survive. To actually compete with large businesses, you need to think as they do and to form strategic alliances with them.

Large businesses understand the national and global market. They realize that access to these markets is vital for their continued growth. They also know that inefficient processes and outdated technologies will cost them money in the end.

It's really no different for a small business. As a business owner you can decide to stay local, but you probably won't stay in business very long. If you sell your product only in your local community, you'll limit growth and profitability. Give your business greater access in your state and country, and you increase the potential for growth and increased revenue. But why settle for that? Why not build a business that can operate globally?

I mentioned in this book that the "dot comers" had the right vision, but lacked the skills to make their vision a reality. Many business owners are in the same situation; they're afraid to even *think* globally, because they don't understand how to do it.

They say everything's easy if you know how to do it. I understand this process because I've done it for major corporations and for my own business. My business currently sells products globally and I do it without any employees. My wife and I run the entire business from our home. The business is extremely profitable and I spend my time enjoying life instead of working around the clock to make a living. The obvious questions are:

- How does one accomplish this?
- How much does it cost?
- How long will it take?

Since I mentioned above that large companies spend millions to globalize, will you need to spend a million dollars? The answer is definitely no. You won't have to spend the money, but you do need to learn certain strategies and understand why each is important. You will also need to develop strategic relationships that will facilitate your growth, but keep your expenses low. As a business owner you need to think like this:

- How can I run my business with the highest profit and the lowest cost?
- How can I expand globally?
- How can I do it without having to work around the clock every day?
- What does it take to build the strategic relationships required to achieve these goals?

Strategic relationships or strategic partnerships should be thought of as relationships where both parties benefit. It isn't the same as having a business partner. A business partner owns part of your business and will have some control over your enterprise. *A strategic partner is an organization that provides a service or benefit to you for a cost.* The cost can be in dollars or discounts. A strategic partner will minimize your cost of entry into a market, because you'll use their network. A chain store with retail outlets throughout the US may be a good strategic partner because by carrying your produce in their store they'll give you immediate national exposure. There will be a cost associated via some type of discount or wholesale pricing, but immediate exposure saves you years of time and lots of money.

Strategic Partners and Their Networks

As a new business on a budget, you'll encounter many closed doors. Your company is new, you have no revenue or history, and your business has no credit. You're a risk to do business with. What you need is someone that can give you credibility and access. Strategic Partners do this for you.

How does this work? Established businesses are always looking for new sources of revenue. In order to grow, they require new products, ideas, or companies that will add value or revenue to their bottom line. Retail store chains seek new products to carry; bookstores need new books; movie producers want new movie ideas; record companies look for new material;

technology companies seek value-added technology. Part of your job is finding companies that provide these products to the end customer or to retailers. Such companies include distributors, wholesalers, or partner firms that have access to a variety of other companies and customers.

You need to create a relationship with these companies, to become a strategic partner with them. With a good amount of research you'll be able to find these companies. Contact them and pursue discussions about their requirements for new products and services. Verify that they have a pipeline to the organizations and customer groups you want to reach. Structure deals with them that allow them to offer your product to retailers, end customers, or other distributors. By doing this you automatically become a part of their product offering and gain immediate access to their network.

This approach saves months and years of trying to build a similar network. You should find as many partners as possible like this. Learn who the major retailers are for your type of product and find out which distributors they order from. Make every effort to build a relationship with these distributors. You'll have a difficult time selling directly to a large retailer, but if your product is a part of an offering from a distributor they trust, the product will be easily accepted. By using an established distribution network, your product becomes immediately legitimate. Using an existing network is clearly a preferred choice for various reasons, including:

- You take advantage of pre-established relationships
- This path has already been paved, tried, tested, and proven.
- Once you're a part of the network, you'll gain access to different areas of the network
- It's the quickest way to reach and access your target market.
- You can use as many networks as necessary to build your business.

- You can sell mass quantities of your product through distributors.

Retail vs. Wholesale

When you sell your product, you have a choice of selling retail or wholesale. You should choose both. When selling retail, you receive a marked-up value for your product. However, the cost of building a retail network is very expensive. Also your ability to sell a mass quantity of retail products is limited by your lack of funds. It could cost hundreds of thousands or millions in retail space, equipment, sales, advertising, and marketing to sell your products directly to consumers on a large scale. Even if you sell retail on the Internet without office space, the cost of marketing to build a trusted brand will be prohibitive.

One reason the Internet boom failed was because techies who could create beautiful web sites didn't understand the economics of retail business. Having a web site saved the cost of a storefront, but customers will only buy from trusted sources – and most people don't trust the Internet. People will purchase from brands they recognize, such as amazon.com, because a vast amount of money was spent building these brands. The same products sold at rohanhall.com won't sell as well; not because there isn't enough traffic, but because rohanhall.com wasn't recommended by a trusted source and isn't a household name. The largest cost of building an online retail business is marketing the brand to build the trust and confidence of potential customers.

Various studies report the millions of dollars required to build a trusted brand. As a new, small business you probably don't have millions to spend on marketing your website. We'll discuss marketing in a later chapter and show you some ways you can build your brand without spending tons of money.

In comparison, when you sell your products to distributors or retailers, you create a different situation. You're actually relying on *their* trusted brand – a brand they've spent huge sums of money to build. A customer will buy your product from amazon.com or Macys without knowing who actually created the product. They buy it because these retail outlets have already established a trusted relationship with them, based on performance and huge marketing budgets.

A customer with the choice of buying your product on your website or buying it on the website of a known retailer will choose the known retailer most of the time, even if the price is slightly less on your website.

Likewise, retailers will more easily buy from wholesalers and distributors they have a relationship with, instead of buying directly from you. This reduces the number of vendors they have to work with, which also reduce their risk and cost.

Therefore, you will need to introduce your product at the level of distributors.

Selling as a retailer
- More cost to sell products
- More revenue per sale

Selling as a wholesaler
- Less cost to sell product
- Less revenue per sale (because of discounts)
- More sales volume

Product Flow

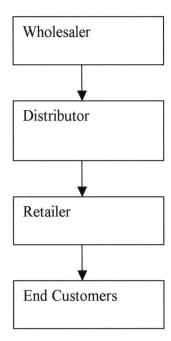

I will explain more about these types of relationships in future chapters. However, before we can build a business we'll need to start the business and create products.

Rohan Hall

Section II

Build your Agile Business Structure

Rohan Hall

Chapter 3

Starting a Business

————————

Starting a business today only takes a few minutes of your time. You don't need attorneys to file expensive documents. Everything you need to start a business in the United States is free and online. Of the various countries I've worked in, I have not found another country that makes starting a business easier.

Even though you have different decisions regarding what type of business, stocks, partnership options etc, the actual process of starting a business in the USA has only two steps. The steps are:

1. Register your business entity in the state(s) of your choosing
2. Register the business entity with the federal government (Form SS-4)

Register your business with a State

To register your business, you'll need to file one or more documents required by the state. The easiest way to do this is to log onto your state's web site, find the document required for the business type you're trying to create, and then fill out the required form and submit it. You'll be able to accomplish this online or download it from the web site. The site will provide specific instruction on what to do, which documents to file, and any fees you need to pay. The different types of business entities are listed in this chapter.

Each state has a website with a similar format that includes the state's name. For example:

- Florida: www.florida.gov
- Nevada: www.nevada.gov
- Texas: www.texas.gov
- Georgia: www.gorgia.gov.
- and so on!

Some states abbreviate their website address by the state's abbreviation. Currently, there is no www.california.gov, but there is a www.ca.gov. Some have both, such as Missouri, which has both www.mo.gov and www.missouri.gov. You may have to try both formats to find your state.

For every rule, there are exceptions. New York, for instance, does not use the .gov extension. If you can't find your state, you may need to do an Internet search, using the keywords *mystate government.* For instance, type "New York State government" or "New York State .gov" in an Internet search engine to find the New York State website.

The important thing to remember is that the .gov extension is the official extension used by governments. If you use a .com extension you may find a commercial website. The .gov website will be updated and maintained by the government and contains the most accurate information. The information will also be free, paid for by your tax dollars. You may also find websites with a .org, .net or some other extension. These websites are probably created by a private firm or individual and may charge for information you can obtain free on the .gov websites. The .gov websites focus on providing official state-related information and assistance.

Stop Working!

Once you locate your state's web site, look for the link that takes you to the business section. The link may be labeled Business, Starting a Business, or Doing Business in our state. The word *Business* will most likely be a part of the label. Read the information provided by the state. Each state will have different laws that govern how you do business in that state. You may need to be aware of certain licenses, fees, or taxes. Most state web sites give more details that you'll ever need. Be sure and read the FAQ (Frequently Asked Questions) section – it summarizes the most vital points.

If you plan to have an attorney help with starting your business, read the details from your state's web site *before* talking with the attorney. Then you'll be more informed, which will save you money in the long run.

If you've decided to do this yourself, then you need to understand what forms to fill out. The forms are driven by the type of business you plan to start.

In addition to the other websites, the IRS (Internal Revenue Service) has an amazingly informative web site. The site provides comprehensive tax information, plus a variety of links to various state and government websites. One such link is http://www.irs.gov/businesses/small/article/0,,id=99021,00.html. This page links you directly to information about doing business in each state. You'll find this page hold valuable information you need to do business in a particular state. If this page becomes unavailable at sometime in the future you can always navigate from the www.irs.gov main webpage to new information they have regarding this subject matter. The IRS website is an excellent resource for a variety of state and federal questions you may have about your business.

Before starting a business in the state of your choice, you need to determine the type of business structure you plan to use. Each structure has advantages and disadvantages based on risk and taxation. According to the IRS website:

The most common forms of business are the sole proprietorship, partnership, corporation, and S corporation. A more recent twist to these forms of business is the introduction of the Limited Liability Company (LLC) or the Limited Liability Partnership (LLP).

*A **sole proprietorship** is an unincorporated business that is owned by one individual. It is the simplest form of business organization to start and maintain. The business has no existence apart from you, the owner. Its liabilities are your personal liabilities and you undertake the risks of the business for all assets owned, whether used in the business or personally owned. You include the income and expenses of the business on your own tax return.*

*A **partnership** is the relationship existing between two or more persons who join to carry on a trade or business. Each person contributes money, property, labor, or skill, and expects to share in the profits and losses of the business.*

A partnership is not a taxable entity. Each partner includes his or her share of the partnership's income or loss on his or her tax return.

*In forming a **corporation** , prospective shareholders transfer money, property, or both, for the corporation's capital stock. A corporation generally takes the same deductions as a sole proprietorship to compute its taxable income. A corporation can also take special deductions.*

The profit of a corporation is taxed to both the corporation and to the shareholders when the profit is distributed as dividends. However, shareholders cannot deduct any loss of the corporation.

*An eligible domestic corporation can avoid double taxation (once to the shareholders and again to the corporation) by electing to be treated as **an S corporation** . An S corporation generally is exempt from federal income tax. Its shareholders include on their tax returns their share of the corporation's separately stated items of income, deduction, loss, and credit, and their share of nonseparately stated income or loss.*

***An LLC and/or LLP** makes an entity election with Form 8832, Entity Classification Election. An LLC may be a sole proprietorship, a corporation, or a partnership. (A minimum of two members is required for federal tax purposes to operate an LLC as a partnership.) Consequently, the applicable tax forms, estimated tax payment requirements, and related tax publications depend upon whether the LLC operates as a sole proprietorship, corporation, or partnership. The default entity for federal tax treatment of an LLC with two or more members is a partnership. The default entity of an LLP is a partnership and the partnership tax forms, estimated tax payment requirements, and partnership publications apply.*[2]

Many new businesses use an S-Corporation structure, which gives you the protection of a Corporation with the flexibility of a Sole Proprietorship. Additionally, you avoid double taxation. However, you should speak to your accountant for advice regarding which business structure is best for the business you'll be starting.

---

[2] Source http://www.irs.gov/businesses/small/article/0,,id=98359,00.html

Register the business entity with the federal government

You will need to register your business and receive an Employer Identification Number (EIN) from the federal government by using Form SS-4, unless you're doing business as a Sole Proprietor.

For businesses, the EIN is similar to your social security number. It's used during all your business communications with the government. Creditors and vendors will require it for payments and some customers also require it. Banks will ask for this number when you open a business account, and you'll need it when you pay taxes. It's also required when registering the business with your state.

Many state web sites now have links to the IRS web site, where you can apply for this number. You should read the state's website carefully however because some of them have a delay of up to two weeks in getting you this important number. However, there's no need to wait because you can get it immediately online at http://www.irs.gov/businesses/small/article/0,,id=97860,00.html or by calling the IRS at (800) 829-4933. You can also download the form at www.irs.gov/pub/irs-pdf/fss4.pdf. The IRS link for general EIN information is http://www.irs.gov/businesses/small/article/0,,id=98350,00.html.

Getting Started

Now that you've started your business, you'll need to know a variety of things as you get started. Naturally, you will want to keep the cost as low as possible as you go forward, but there are certain things you can't do without because they're invaluable to building your infrastructure. On the other hand, there are things you shouldn't spend money on – at least initially. These are nice-to-have elements, but they don't make an immediate contribution to your business.

Stop Working!

You need a computer

Computers are never cheap, but they're less expensive now that ever before. I suggest you invest in a computer if you don't already own one. Buy the cheapest new computer you can find. I suggest a new one, because computers become obsolete in about 3 years. You can use a computer for about five years, but the software changes often. If you buy an old computer, it's probably already obsolete and you'll have a difficult time finding compatible software.

To find the best deal, shop around on the Internet and look for sales in your local newspaper. The Sunday papers offer lots of sales on technology equipment. If you aren't comfortable with computers, go into a computer store and ask as many questions as possible to get a better understanding. Typically, the basic model on sale will be enough for most new businesses.

You need a bank account

In addition to starting the company, you also need to open a bank account, but first you'll need an Employee Identification Number (EIN) for the bank to use. You may want to memorize this number, because you'll use it a lot. All your banking, business, and tax transactions, will tie back to this EIN.

Banking technology and business processes

A common theme you'll read throughout this book is the huge investment banks, corporate business, and the federal and state governments have made in improving their business processes and technologies. Many people don't care about this because they don't really understand how to use this investment to their benefit. One of the most direct ways to extend and globalize your business is to find ways to use other companies' investment into technology and business processes to your advantage. I'll show you how to do this throughout the book.

Banks will track each transaction you make with them, and they've always done so. What has changed over the last few years is their ability to give you access to this information This becomes a valuable asset for managing your books and paying bills. Instead of waiting around for paper statements every month and spending hours reconciling your bank account, you can obtain online access to this information. Furthermore, with online banking you'll gain the ability to download these transactions to your favorite financial software, such as Quicken, QuickBooks, MS Money or any other brand of financial software. Additionally, instead of writing a check, finding a stamp, addressing an envelope, and mailing it, you can do the entire thing online. It's safe, it's effective, and most of all – it's free.

So how can you use this to your advantage? First, start a small business account with a national bank. The things you should require from them include:

- online statements
- the ability to download transactions
- the ability to pay bills online
- check cards.

I picked a national bank because they typically have a greater investment in technology, and I use their investment to help run my business. Smaller banks normally have much better service when you go into the bank but I rarely every go to the bank except to deposit checks. Unfortunately, the United States is significantly behind with direct deposit technology. I prefer to have my checks directly deposited but many businesses still struggle with this simple concept. Comparatively, this is standard technology for business in Europe, Asia and much of the world.

Once you start a business account you should never mix personal and business bank account transactions. Use your business account only for business. If you mix them it will make your life challenging, especially when it comes to doing your taxes.

When you open your bank account, make sure you sign up for Internet access to your account so you can download your bank transactions to one of the standard financial applications as mentioned above. Choose the product you prefer, but make sure you buy the business version of the software. Each of these products does basically the same thing: they allow you to manage your business financial transactions with different levels of complexity. Whatever software you choose, be sure it can process business financial statements with the data you import. This is very important and it can save you tons of time and money. Imagine if you had to manually enter every transaction into your financial software? Yes, I know that's what most people do right now. I don't. It takes me five minutes or less to enter all my financial transactions for any given month into my financial software. I can do 10 transactions or 5000 within the same length of time. The entire process takes a few minutes or seconds – and it's completely error free. The current versions of some financial software will even do the download automatically without your intervention. I never have to worry about typos, errors, or missed transactions. Also, reconciling my accounts each month is significantly easier. I simply run some standard reports and compare them to my bank statement, which is also online. Since the source of the downloaded data and the bank statements are the same, the need for reconciliation is practically eliminated – unless I have transactions from other sources, such as credit cards or other bank accounts.

Also, because your software comes with the ability to produce financial statements, you don't need to know how to create these statements. You just need to know how to execute them in your application. The application will use the data you imported to create statements such as cash flow, revenue/expenses, a balance sheet, and a variety of other statements you or your accountant will need to manage your financial position and your taxes.

I also like banks that keep their transactions online for at least 6 months. I prefer a year or more, because I may be busy on vacation or traveling on business for a month or two and I want to be able to download data when I get back home. Banks that have transactions online for only a month make this difficult. I'd have to alter my lifestyle because of their software.

I also like an online help feature my particular bank has: they let customers ask email questions from online accounts. This could be an inquiry about an invalid charge on my account, how to get new checks, how to use features of the online system, or any other bank-related question. They get back to you within 24 hours. Of course, I can also pick up the phone and call them if I want. But since I'm a technical type of guy and may have questions at 3:00 AM from some remote part of the world, I can simply log onto my account from my computer or an internet café, post a question, and check back the next day for a response. I've done that before and it's a great service.

I have a business check book, but I try to pay all my bills online because it's free and efficient. I set up my vendors with the bank software, the software links to my checking account, and I authorize how much money I want to pay to whom. I do this for personal as well as business expenses, and the banking software keeps these transactions separate for me. Most banking online payment software also allows electronic bills to be displayed online. This is a move away from the paper bills you receive in the mail. You have full control of this process. No money will be paid to your vendors unless you authorize each individual payment. You can pay any vendor or individual this way. You can send money to your sister or pay your accountant for services performed. You can also schedule recurring payments for loans or mortgages if you want to.

I like online banking because banks spent a lot of money on this technology and I reap the benefits of their investment. I've rarely found going into a bank a pleasant experience, and I hate dealing with long lines and incompetent clerks. I also resent sitting at my desk opening bills, writing checks, finding envelopes, licking stamps, and driving to the post office just to send money to someone in the mail. It feels archaic to me. The same way email replaced the need to write and post letters is the way online bill payment will replace hand-written checks. When was the last time you actually wrote a letter and posted it when you had the option to send an email? It will soon be like that for online bill payment.

But don't throw away your checkbook. There are times when I need to hand a check to someone standing in front of me, but this doesn't happen more than a few times per year. I do everything possible online.

The bank must also offer me a free Check Card. The difference between a Check Card and a credit card is the difference between no financial control and good financial control. I keep a credit card for emergencies. (My credit card company must also give me the option to download my transactions). I do practically everything else with my Check Card, because it keeps me honest with myself. Credit cards let me pretend I can afford to do things that I really can't. For instance, I may want to spend $5,000 on an item and just pull out my credit card because I have a $20,000 available balance. However, the Check Card takes the money directly from my bank account, so I feel a more immediate impact. Instead of spending that $5000, I would do more research to see if I could find a less expensive approach to my purchase.

Another difference between Check Cards and credit cards is that most people take months or years to pay off credit card balances. This drives you into debt and makes you a slave of the credit card company. You go to work to pay the debt instead of going to work to finance your business and your retirement. I use my disposable income to finance my business and long term wealth, not to pay off debt. I've had massive debt before and I never want to walk that path again.

Also, Check Cards are valuable for people who don't have perfect credit. With most banks, everyone qualifies for a Check Card when you open a checking account. But not everyone qualifies for a credit card. Check Cards can be used exactly the same as credit cards, with very few exceptions. They're typically issued as Visa Check Cards. If you have a credit problem, you can use this as a Visa card and no one will be the wiser. If you take a client out for dinner they'll see the Visa symbol and assume you're using a credit care. You can also buy items online with your Check Card. You just have to make sure you always have enough funds in the bank account to cover your charges.

By using the bank's technology, things that would take hours of your time now take only a few minutes every month. And the great thing about it is you won't need to pay a bookkeeper or accountant to do any of it. My accountant only needs to review and certify my books and help me file my taxes. So I not only save time, I also save money.

Optimized Banking Business Processes

OLD – Bill Payment	NEW – Bill Payment
Receive bill from vendor	Receive bill or schedule payment online
Write paper checks	Click Approve
Find stamp (or buy)	Click Send
Lick/seal envelop with payment	
Go to mailbox	
Post	
Balance checkbook	
Record vendor invoice in books	
Record vendor payment in books	
Record new account balance	

OLD – Invoice/Receive Cash	NEW – Invoice/Receive Cash
Create invoice for customer	Create electronic invoice
Find stamp (or buy)	Email invoice to customer
Lick/seal envelop with invoice	Deposit checks or receive direct deposit
Go to mailbox	
Post	

Record invoice transaction in books	
Receive Payment from customer	
Deposit check(s)	
Record cash receipt transaction in books	

OLD – Monthly Reconciliation	NEW – Monthly Reconciliation
Receive bank statement	Download transactions to financial software
Review paper invoice, checks, records	View various pre-designed financial reports from financial software.
Compare with bank statement	
Correct errors	
Create financial reports as desired	

As you can see, with online banking you've optimized your business process dramatically. Your time optimization will be even more noticeable.

Instead of being buried under tons of paper at the end of every day or spending weekend time managing your books, all you have to do is download the transactions as frequently as you like. The software contains prepackaged reports that show your revenue, expenses, and current balances. You won't have to calculate anything. You don't even need to know accounting or how to balance your checkbook. A later chapter will teach you some basic accounting skills so you'll understand the primary reports. Whenever you meet with your accountant, all you have to do is print the statements and show them to him. If the accountant is up to date with technology, you should be able to export the transactions and email them to him or her.

The bank spent millions of dollars to develop this technology. By having a relationship with them, you get to use that technology to your benefit without the cost.

This is what it will cost you for this error free, efficient financial business structure. It's a one-time investment and it's tax deductible:

Technological Infrastructure	Investment Dollars
Computer	$500
Printer, Scanner, Fax combo	$150
Financial Software	$100
24 hour account access	$0
Online statements	$0
Online bill payment	$0
Check Card	$0
24 hour online help	$0
	===========
Total Technology Investment	$750

So, once you've started your business, invest in a computer, create a new bank account, and set up your banking process. You've now completed the first step towards building your business.

Show Me the Money

Starting A Business
========

Anyone can give you his or her opinion and vague ideas about how to start a business or get rich. I really, really hate that! I'm also insulted by people who think I need to be motivated to get rich or I need to work harder. Trust me, I'm motivated and I've worked hard my entire life without exception. What I always wanted to know is *exactly* can I do to get rich, and how did other people do it? It clearly doesn't happen just through hard work. The poorest people I know are the hardest workers. It's not due to lack of education alone, because I know well-educated people who are poor. What I always wanted to know was how the authors of these self-help books made their money and exactly how they built their financial organizations.

At the end of each chapter I'll tell you exactly how my companies are structured, how they make money, who some of my strategic partners are, and how each segment of this book applies to my own businesses. In other words, you get the concepts, *and* you learn how to apply them to your own business. The two businesses I'll focus on are Eye Contact Media, Inc. and vConcepts, Inc.

Fair enough?

Eye Contact Media, Inc. (www.eyecontactmedia.com)
If you look on the cover of this book you'll see that it was published by Eye Contact Media, Inc. I have 100% ownership of this company. It's a new company I started about a year ago. I began this business to prove a concept: your small business can compete in the market with any multinational business – and produce enough cash flow so you can stop working.

I wanted to illustrate it was possible to build a company and make it a global player in less than a year. I built it with the structure in the flowcharts above. I created an Agile organization. Within a few months of starting the business and releasing our first product, customers all over the world were buying our product. In the first year of operations we gained customers in the United States, Europe, Asia, South America, Australia and a variety of other countries.

Eye Contact Media takes advantage of various global strategic partnerships and networks. There are currently no employees. There are no immediate plans for employees. We have no debt. We have a constant positive flow of revenue. My wife and I spend a few minutes per day managing the business. Our greatest management tools are email and the Internet. We use email for 99% of our communications. We use the Internet to access our strategic partners' technology and do research. We do tons of research on every potential partner and idea we think about pursuing. We own no warehouse, but our products are warehoused all over the world. We have no manufacturing plants, but our products are produced with the highest quality and the lowest cost. We have no employees, but through carefully selected strategic partnerships, we have some of the best and brightest people working for us every day of the week.

The company is well marketed, with increased sales every month. We have no marketing or sales staff. The business appears to *run itself.* In reality, it does run itself. This book is our second product. We'll talk about our first product in the chapter on *Products.*

What makes Eye Contact Media unique is that it cost us virtually nothing to start and a minimum investment to operate. We had no investors, loans or debt in starting and operating this business. The company pays for itself, was profitable from the beginning, and will always be profitable. I can say that with confidence because I understand the money. The chapter on Money and Finance will give you the same level of confidence about your business as well.

Stop Working!

Eye Contact Media is an expression of the Agile Business concept. Our infrastructure is built on the infrastructure of Mega Organizations and other business entities, using their global access and relationships – leaving us free to focus on our core competencies (the things we do best). We're able to focus on business strategy; product strategy and creation, and relationship building. This takes only a few minutes per day of effort between my wife and myself.

Since our partners are performing all the other daily business tasks, we can stop working whenever we want, while the business continues to generate cash. Or we can continue introducing more products to grow the business even larger. Since we aren't part of the daily core business processes, this gives us a lot of personal freedom to enjoy life. If we decide to do some traveling, there's no impact on the business. We can go away for a month or more and the business will continue to operate. The business functions like an independent, living entity. It continues growing everyday; it never sleeps, it never gets tired, and it takes no vacations. It's a well oiled, money-making machine.

Starting Eye Contact Media

It took us only a few minutes to start the company. Articles of Incorporation and an application for Employee Identification Number were all we needed. We did everything online. The state and federal governments have caught up with technology over the last few years. We didn't use an attorney for any of this. We simply logged onto our state's web site and the IRS website to submit the appropriate forms. That's all it took.

Costs to start Eye Contact Media were:

Item	Cost
State Articles of Incorporation Filing Fee	$87.50
Federal Filing fee	$0
Total	*$87.50*

Computer

I already own a Windows XP and Windows 2000 computer. I didn't need another computer. I also already own financial software, so I didn't need to buy one. I did purchase a printer-fax-scanner combo product for about $125 for this business.

My initial technology investment for Eye Contact Media was as follows:

Technological Infrastructure	Investment Dollars
Computer	$0
Printer, Scanner, Fax combo	$125
Financial Software	$0
24 hour account access	$0
Online statements	$0
Online bill payment	$0
Check Card	$0
24 hour online help	$0
==========	
Total Technology Investment	$125

Banking

I did exactly what was presented above. I started a business account with a national bank that gave me access to all the technology I needed for effective financial business processes. I log onto our bank account at will from anywhere in the world. I pay my bills from anywhere in the world. I use my Check Card for all expenses I don't write checks for. On a monthly basis I download all our financial transactions from the bank to our financial software – a process I'm now automating to occur daily without my intervention. The software is delivered with various financial reports I use to see the position of my business. This process takes only a few minutes per month.

Stop Working!

vConcepts, Inc (www.vconceptsinc.com)
I started vConcepts years ago. This is my software consulting company and we specialize in implementing ERP applications. I've worked very hard at this company. vConcepts' clients include various Fortune companies, and I've spent years helping these clients become more efficient and competitive locally, nationally, and globally.

I mentioned some of the work I've done for clients earlier in this book, but the core body of my work has always been the optimization of business processes with technology. Through this work, companies have become more efficient and competitive in their market by streamlining their corporate supply/demand chain, manufacturing, and financial processes. These processes are then integrated throughout the entire organization, including partners and customers.

vConcepts was started in a similar manner to Eye Contact Media, although at the time it wasn't as easy to do many of the things I discuss in this book online. For instance, the Articles of Incorporation and the S-44 Federal EIN forms weren't available online. In those days, the Internet was just a buzzword in tech magazines. Enterprise resource planning (ERP) had just started taking off. We used another type of technology called client/server technology to accomplish some of the things we now do effortlessly with the Internet. Companies had just begun to make massive investments in their infrastructures. I'd already been involved in technology for over 10 years and saw great potential for the integration of enterprises – I'd been doing it already, but in a different way. Instead of having technology do the integration, other technologist and I were actually *writing* technologies to do the integration.

Therefore, the first time I saw technology that could standardize what we were trying to create, it was in instant sell. It simply made sense. The major software companies doing this kind of work at the time were SAP AG, a German company that's still the leader in the market; PeopleSoft, an American company that's now #2 in the market; Oracle, another American company that became famous from it's database technology; and BAAN, a Dutch company that has since lost its market position.

Companies spent billions of dollars collectively on these technologies in order to integrate their enterprises. Companies also developed various internal technologies to achieve the same goal.

Having a background of developing these types of client/server and database technologies, I decided to apply this knowledge to enterprise resource planning via vConcepts. vConcepts continues to do this type of work today with a variety of clients.

Banking

vConcepts currently use the same banking features as Eye Contact Media, gaining all the same advantages. It takes me minutes per month to do the corporate financial statements. It took less than an hour to do both companies' end-of-year financial statements for last year. I simply forwarded the information to my accountant so he could complete my taxes. This streamlined process also helps reduce errors with IRS filings, because the data being submitted was downloaded and collected directly from the bank and processed with an off-the-shelf standard financial application.

Chapter 4

Your Product

Now that you have your company started, you need to sell something. That item or service is your product.

When you think of your product, you should smile. You should smile because you believe you're about to fulfill a need in the marketplace. Remember, your product will be half the reason you become rich. Your strategic focus and networking are the other half.

In your Agile organization, your products will be one of your primary assets. They will bring the constant and indefinite cash flow that will make you rich. Eventually you'll create multiple products to improve your asset position. However, first you should focus on just one product to introduce to the market.

Introducing that first product to your Agile organization is important in multiple ways. First, the initial produce will test your Agile network. It will tell you how efficient your network gives you access to the customers you want to reach.

You shouldn't try to release multiple products at the start of your business. First you should release your initial product, test your network, collect feedback about the product and your network, and then make improvements as needed. Only after you have fully tested your product and your network should you release additional products. This minimizes the potential cost of releasing multiple products in an untested network structure.

To ensure a good product release you should spend a lot of time thinking about what the product should look like, feel like, taste like, and smell like. It should be important enough for you to do lots of research about this product. You should know what makes your product different than any other product in the market. Why should someone spend his or her money on this product? Who are your primary competitors in the market? It doesn't have to be a unique product, but it must have something that makes it different from other products in the market.

Look around, see what other people are doing, and see if you can find a way to do it better. You'll probably be disappointed in trying to be totally original. If you think you have something that no one has ever done before, it's probably because you haven't done enough research. Plus, why try to invent the wheel when all you need to do is improve upon it?

You should also think of what you already know how to do. The most cost efficient product you can sell is one you make yourself. You should productize your knowledge and skills. What are people paying you to do now? Is there a way you can use this skill to create a product? If you get paid now to perform a professional service, can you convert that knowledge into a product? Can you buy the rights to a product someone else has created and improve it?

A success icon I practically grew up with is Bill Gates. No, we weren't in the same neighborhood, but we grew up during the same technological revolution the 80s, 90s, and now the millennium. What has always impressed me about Bill Gates and

Microsoft is that I'm not aware of any product they *invented*, though they developed various technologies. Yet they're the biggest and best in one of the most competitive industries in the world.

My first interaction with Microsoft was with my first company when I assembled and sold computers at 19 years old. The first time I used Microsoft's MS DOS, I thought "Hey, this is like CPM!" CPM at the time was an operating system similar to MS DOS. Additionally, according to the stories, Gates didn't write MS DOS – he simply bought the rights to the technology from someone else.

Gates apparently improved on the product he now owned and converted it into the dominant software product in the world. There was nothing really interesting or fascinating about the technology. It had some improvements that let it work better with IBM's new Personal Computer, but that was it. Functionally and technically, to my recollection, it did the same things CPM or any other operating system of the time did. Gates had the first piece of the puzzle – the product. The second piece was IBM's network that he tapped into. Gates' strategic focus made MS DOS the standard for computer users everywhere.

Years later, Microsoft released other technologies that had simple improvements over other existing technologies. Some of these include:

Microsoft Products	Other Product
MS DOS	CPM
MS ACCESS	DBASE
MS WORD	Word Star, Word Perfect
MS Windows	Apple, Xerox
MS Excel	Lotus 123, Supercalc, Visicalc
MS Internet Explorer	Netscape Navigator
Windows NT/2000	VAX VMS

Microsoft didn't try to invent the wheel; they simply gave it better traction. Microsoft isn't the only company to do this.

Many companies become wealthy by making slight improvements over existing products and using a network and strategic relationships to take advantage of this differentiator.

So when you design your product, originality and creativity are good, but focus on something that will sell and has specific things that make it different from other products in the market.

After you create your first product and put it into a network for sales and distribution, you'll have the opportunity to introduce other products. The important goal is to have products with an unlimited capacity to reproduce and sell, plus a network that allows you to sell to a mass market at a reasonable profit.

Intellectual Property

You probably already have in mind the kind of product you'd like to manufacture and sell. You have an infinite number of choices and opportunities to select from.

Even though you can use an Agile structure for virtually any type of product, my personal preference is a product that gives me intellectual property ownership. Such products can often be created with little cost. For instance, I can write a book or make a music CD. The moment I create these products I'm protected by the government for the rest of my life – and longer – from people illegally copying and distributing my work. I also like software technology. Even if you're not a programmer, you can do what is called a *work for hire,* whereby you pay someone to develop your idea. You own all intellectual property rights to the final product and you can duplicate and sell this product for as long as you want to.

I like several other things about intellectual property products. For one thing, manufacturing and distributing these products is usually inexpensive. You can also create the product and sell it in various types of media: print, electronic, tapes, etc.

Some Examples of Intellectual Property
• Books

Stop Working!

- Music
- Movies
- Computer Software

Your greatest challenge will be to develop the product, something you probably enjoy doing anyway.

If you doubt the value of intellectual property, simply look at the entertainment industry and the technology industry. Can you imagine the massive amount of wealth in one room at the Grammy awards or the Academy awards? How do you think they make their money? How can one actor be paid 30 million dollars for one film? They make that kind of money because it's cheaper for studios to pay them $30 million than to give him residual rights to the movie. The really big moneymakers aren't the actors – it's the studio owners, because they own the intellectual property.

Consider the music industry. Entertainers make an incredible amount of money, but not like the executives who *own* the entertainment companies. Over the last 10 years I've watched music executives take advantage of the new Hip-Hop music. Many of these executives started out in ghettos and had little or no access to capital when they started their organizations. Now they flaunt millions and a lifestyle that's shown constantly on entertainment programs once reserved for top Hollywood moneymakers. Many of these music producers have also been featured in financial magazines such as Fortune Magazine, Inc, Forbes and a variety of other business magazines. Some of these executives include Sean Combs (P. Ditty), Percy Miller (Master P.), Andre Young (Dr. Dre), and Russell Simmons.

If you haven't heard about these men, then I'm sure your children have. They identified a market, built intellectual property based products to take advantage of this market. They then used strategic relationships and global distribution channels to become extremely wealthy. They sell to a global market, not a local market. You can hear hip-hop on radio stations and nightclubs in Tokyo, Rome, Paris, Amsterdam, Thailand, the

Bahamas, Hong Kong and other countries all over the world as easily as you do in the United States. This is not ghetto music, this is a globalize business.

Entrepreneurs in the technology market did the same thing. They built products to take advantage of emerging markets coupled with good business processes and a network through which they sold their products. Michael Dell (Dell Computers), Bill Gates (Microsoft), and Jeff Besos (Amazon.com) are some of the more popular successes in the technology market. Their companies own a variety of intellectual properties that have made them rich.

All these people are inspirational. They are self-made millionaires and billionaires. They own intellectual property products and used strategic relationships to become incredibly wealthy.

Business Meets Creativity

It always bothers me when people talk about the left brain versus the right brain. I think that's nonsense. To box someone into a category of being creative or not creative is simply hogwash. I think everyone has a creative spirit, but we all express it differently.

I like intellectual property creation because it allows me to express myself creatively in order to support my business. I find writing computer code to be as creative as writing a book. Both require structure and the creative expression of ideas. There's also the satisfaction of building something from nothing. The transformation process is inspiring and the completion is fulfilling.

Building your product can be fun and expressive. You have no boss and only self-imposed deadlines. You are the boss, the judge, and the critic. The market will be the final decision-maker, but you have some control over that as well. However, you may find that you become your worst critic. That's good; it means that you're applying high standards to your creation. After all, in the end, you'll have only yourself to blame for your success or failures.

If you create your own product you may discover something interesting: You keep all the profits. The numbers will speak for themselves. You can work for someone and receive a salary, or you can work for yourself and keep all the profits. Many artists work very hard, only to hand the majority of their profits to a record studio or publisher. Don't blame the record label or publisher – you handed them your work and asked them to keep the profits. Do it for yourself and you'll never have those conflicts again!

I have a friend that did this recently. He had a baby and found that he wanted to share the experience of raising his child with his family, his wife's family, and their friends. They live in a different city than their families and wanted to make sure that they could share the experience with others as their child grows.

He found email to be limited and there were a lot of free online websites to share photos but they didn't have the personalized factors that he wanted to share. So he built his own website to do it. For many people, just having a website to share pictures would be enough. This guy is the Super Dad type though. He's crazy about his new son and really wanted to capture and share each special moment. So he built the site to show photos, video clips, audio for the first sounds, a growth chart, and a baby journal. Even if you're on the other side of the planet you could see the baby's first step and hear his first words. It was an amazing creation. After awhile I said, "Dude, this is a product". Clearly, I was not the only one who told him this. He went back to working on his site and what evolved from it was a company that allows users to share all the personal details of their baby's experience online. The site is www.babysites.com. It's a full featured website that gives his customers the ability to share personalized information about their babies with anyone in the world that they want to. It's truly a great site and you should check it out especially if you have a baby.

Of course, one of my favorite points to make about intellectual property is the long-term wealth factor. You work once but get paid forever. Not just that, but your children and grandchildren will benefit as well. What a great gift to leave behind after living well from your creations!

Look at Elvis Presley: He's been gone for quite a long time now, but his records still play all over the world and the people with rights to those songs are making money every day. How about books written decades ago? One of my favorite books of all time, *How to Win friends and Influence People* by Dale Carnegie is on the top 100 list of books being sold *today*. This book is so old that when I first got it I was in high school. I got it from my parents and they bought it when they were still pretty young. It's an excellent book and will probably outlast all of us, but the point is that the owners of that intellectual property are still making a killing years after the creator passed away.

If you don't have the skills or time required to create your own intellectual property, then you can either purchase a product someone has already developed or pay someone to develop the product for you. You will need an attorney to protect your rights if you do this.

Know your Market

You will need to do an extensive amount of research about your product market. Is your market domestic only, or international? How large is this market financially? What do similar products like yours sell for in your market? What are the top competing products? What is the demographic of potential customers in this market? Who will you target based on income, race, culture, education, and financial status? Will your products be sold to men, women, or both? What age will these customers be? What language do they speak? What income category will they fall into?

These things are all important. Trying to sell a ten thousand-dollar computer to people who can't afford it is a waste of time. You won't be successful. What if you release a product that targets a certain group, but they find the material religious or racially offensive because you didn't do your research?

Many companies have failed because they took a casual approach to what their market needed and focused more on their personal needs. Because the market drives our economy, you'd do well to understand the market before venturing down this business path.

Know your Competitors

It's virtually impossible to avoid competition when you sell your products. If you find none, then you haven't looked hard enough. You have to understand who these competitors are and which ones are leaders in this particular area. You also need to know why they're successful.

You'll often be asked what makes your product different from these top performers, and you need to give the answer without hesitation.

You can probably find information about your competitors on the Internet. In other cases, you may have to purchase your competitor's product and analyze what's good about it and what needs improvement. You should become an expert on their products, how they do business, their product cost, and their product advantages and disadvantages. As you promote, market, and sell your products, knowing your competitors will give you an advantage.

Product Value

What benefit will I receive from buying your product? Why is it important for me to buy this product today? Why should I not buy your competitor's product? What makes your product better than anything else in the market? When will I receive my return on investment in this product?

These are questions that define the value of your product. You'll have to spend time documenting these perceived values and communicate them when you market your product. The more value and differentiators you can identify and communicate about your product, the better it will do in the market.

Design

To be an artist is a wonderful thing. When you design your product you're an artist. However, don't forget that you're creating a product you want to sell in the open market.

I have a friend who wrote a book some time ago. The research and the information presented were brilliant. It took years to gather all that data. However, after only a few pages I started getting a headache, because the material was just too complex and difficult to follow. It was boring and you needed an advanced degree in that field to appreciate all the information. Basically, the book was a compilation of research instead of a product for general consumption.

The author was proud of all the research, but the book sold no more than a few copies.

Artists tend to be like that. I work with computer programmers, engineers, and analysts everyday, and the problem is the same. Your work should communicate your ideas. Your design is an expression of that. If your audience can't understand and appreciate your ideas, they won't use or accept your product.

This concept is true for any product you create. A software program should receive the same level of scrutiny from a design point of view as a book or an automobile. You should be aware of things that make the product attractive and things that make it unattractive to those who'll buy and use your product.

Design is extremely important. I love the coffee mug I drank from this morning. It's big, bold, and covered with bright colors. The handle is large enough for my hand and the cup keeps my coffee warm. From a design point of view, it passes the test of usability and attractiveness.

When you design a product, you're looking at two primary things: usability and attractiveness.

Usability is the first item in design and should answer the questions? Will the coffee cup hold the coffee? Will the computer start and execute the applications it is designed to? Will the automobile start and drive from point A to point B? Will the book or movie deliver the story as promised? Have we thought of all the possible functional issues with this design? How can we minimize risks?

Attractiveness is the second item of consideration, and it's equally important. If people don't like your product, they won't buy it or use it. Should we build large or small coffee cups, and what colors or patterns should we use? What operating system should the computer be designed to use? How large should the computer be? What should the computer look like? Should the automobile be sporty, off road, or sleek? What types of automobiles are most popular with the demographics I'm targeting? Should the book or movie be humorous, serious, or factual? Who's the audience for this product?

In the design stage it's important to clarify the detail of how your product should work and what it should look like. A functional product that isn't attractive won't be acceptable to consumers.

Prototype

A prototype is a creation of a functional product based on the design, without the *bells and whistles*. A prototype for a software product may be the product without all the attractiveness features outlined in the design. Prototypes primarily focus on Usability to prove the concept of the design. You create prototypes because doing so takes a fraction of the time it will take to create the finished product. You want to know if the product will work before you invest a large amount of time or money in the concept.

Sometimes an idea sounds brilliant and looks wonderful on paper. A design brings some reality to the idea, but it still isn't proven. The prototype will prove or disprove your concept.

Build Product

Once you've designed and prototyped your product, you're ready to build it, while taking into consideration everything you've learned and researched about your product and the market. This is the actual creation of the product – a product that should appeal to your target market.

Depending on the product and your skills, you may choose to build it yourself or to have someone do it for you. If you outsource the creation of this product, make sure you take the legal steps to retain ownership and protect your creation.

The end result must be a fully functional product that's attractive to your product audience.

Test Product

You should do some level of market segment testing for your product. If you created computer software you should have a range of people test it and give feedback about its functionality and ease of use. If you write a book, you should have an impartial audience review it and incorporate important feedback. If you've created a movie or CD, you should also receive feedback about the end product. Get independent feedback on your product so you can enhance it. This important feedback will increase the likelihood of market acceptance.

Show Me the Money

Products

Eye Contact Media, Inc. (www.eyecontactmedia.com)
We needed a product to launch this new business, so we decided to publish our first book: *The System,* authored by Roy Valentine. The book's main focus is to help guys meet and pick up girls.

The System is now one of our intellectual properties, and its long term potential is outstanding. In fact, within a few months of its publication, it became a best seller in several markets. The book has been accepted throughout a good part of the world as an effective solution to an old problem. It will eventually be translated into multiple languages and re-released to various global networks via our strategic partners.

Product Selection
We chose this product because of its simple step-by-step approach to an age-old problem: How does a guy go out and successfully meet and pick up a girl? A variety of other products addressed that problem, but we felt the key differences in our product and our approach would be attractive to a mass audience. The book concept wasn't new, but the approach was convincing.

Product Release
For the first few months, we released the book to 2 strategic partners who have access to a national network, primarily in the United States. In this way we tested the book's market potential and tested our Agile network. The book sales increased every month with no marketing or promotion effort.

We received only positive feedback about the product from both men and women.

We incorporated customer feedback to improve the product. We also improved our Agile structure by partnering with additional strategic partners. Shortly afterwards, we re-release the book to a global network with additional strategic partners. This release was accompanied with a national marketing effort in North America and Canada. Sales via these new channels increased dramatically. The book had its first best seller listing within 4 months after the second release.

Competitors

We faced a variety of competitors in this market, so we made a comprehensive effort to identify differences between *The System's* approach and the competition. *The System's* clear advantages and differentiators were used successfully in our marketing campaign to launch the new release of the book.

Product Differentiator

Your product doesn't have to be unique, but it must have something that makes it different from your primary competitors. You must always be ready to list at least 3 to 5 of these product differentiators and use them as talking points or selling points as required.

For *The System,* the product differentiators are:

The System	Primary Competing Products
Step by step process to meet girls	Generic dating advice
Teaches how to not get rejected	Assumes massive rejection required to meet a girl
Focus on body language and conversation	Pickup lines

Stop Working!

Product Design & Creation

The product was designed and created by the author based on his own philosophy, experience, and approach to meeting girls. Created for a mass audience, the process can be used and applied by anyone. It's explained in simple terms so anyone can learn how to use it.

More information on The System can be found on our website at www.eyecontactmedia.com.

vConcepts, Inc. (www.vconceptsinc.com)
vConcepts is a professional services company that provides ERP software consulting services to our clients. The company also builds complex technologies. The product example I'll use in this book is for our Globileware product.

Globileware is a futuristic mobile technology suite. With Globileware, you can use your cell phone or Personal Digital Assistant (PDA) to do a majority of the business functions you do at work. You can, for instance, process invoices, pay bills, send emails, enter vendor information, delete transactions, look up customer data, review or update inventory information etc. Globileware allows you to use your mobile device to do this and virtually any other business process regardless of your physical location.

Globileware is a middleware technology, using a graphic user interface along with standard wireless protocols to connect to a corporate system. This gives companies access to their corporate information from anywhere in the world via any Internet-enabled wired or wireless device.

From this, you can visualize a sales person closing a deal on the beach in the Bahamas with a Pina Colada in one hand and a wireless PDA in the other. He closes the sale, updates the corporate system, and ships the product with a few clicks on his PDA between sips of his drink. Globileware makes this scenario a reality.

Another vision is a customer ordering your products online with a few clicks on his cell phone while at the park on Saturday afternoon with the grandchildren. He shows the toy to his grandson on the cell phone before clicking the confirm button, knowing he'll receive the product the next day.

A more recent execution of this type of technology is with soldiers in Iraq or in other remote areas of the world with a wireless device guiding them toward their destination. They have full access to top secret information that's fully encrypted in its point to point transmission. Globileware also provide this capability.

Stop Working!

The nature of wireless technology has now extended the capabilities of powerful computer servers to wireless hand held devices. Globileware is the realization and implementation of this new technological wave.

With the highest security possible, you can now give any customer, partner, vendor, or employee of your choosing wireless access to any of your computer servers. They're able to access this information from any Internet-enabled wireless device of their choosing.

For instance, a sales person in a restaurant can check on his customers or products. The restaurant can be anywhere in the world and the database and application he's connecting to can be anywhere in the world.

Market

Corporations and government institutions are the target audience for this technology. Corporate employees spend more and more time away from the office, and government employees need ongoing access to information while in the field. The inability to access information while away from the office creates inefficiencies and costs a significant amount of money.

Organizations may also choose to offer this access to their customers, vendors, and partners. This is similar to giving secured access to ones computer system via the wired Internet.

Product Design

When computer software is created, a variety of design documents are required that discuss all the expected functionality as well as *look and feel* of the application. Should it take 1 click or 3 clicks to reach a particular screen? Is it acceptable for the search function to take 2 seconds or 20 seconds? Should the corporate logo be on every page or just the intro page?

Very specific design documents were created before prototyping and developing Globileware. The design documents considered the variety of technology protocols available in the current market, as well as emerging protocols.

The software was designed to use any client device that has access to the Internet, regardless of whether the device is wired or wireless. It's even possible to have both wired and wireless access simultaneously.

Globileware was also designed to use any back end system. This means it can be implemented to use any ERP, CRM, SCM or other applications found on a computer server. The application also allows access to any database on all the major operating systems.

The design includes a secured plug and play device as a delivery mechanism. Other products of this type are delivered as code. This plug and play device is pre-configured and can be plugged into any existing network system. Access to the corporate system is therefore immediate and avoids the typical customization and development cycle for this type of product.

Prototype, Development & Testing
The application was designed, prototyped, and developed in the United States. The application was tested globally with various partners.

Product Selection
Considerations for selecting this product included:
- For the customer it increases efficiency, reduces cost, and increases profits
- The wireless protocols ensure extremely secure implementation
- It's futuristic, yet based on current standard technology
- It gives access from any wireless device to any server in existence today via any network protocol
- Its protocols are designed to use technologies that could emerge in the coming years

Companies that implement the Globileware suite will have productive employees, whether the employee is in the office or on the road. The employee doesn't need a laptop and a phone jack to plug into. Any standard cell phone with wireless web access will connect them to the corporate technology backbone. The technology is safe, secure, and easy to use.

Wireless technology is sexy today and will be standard tomorrow. Global wireless technology infrastructures are still being built. More mergers of mobile powerhouses will occur. Competition will force consolidation and creative solutions. When the dust is clear, everything we do now on the desktop computer will be possible from any cell phone. Cell phones may become some hybrid of the PDA. Corporations know this and have already begun securing budgets for this emerging revolution. Various government agencies have also invested in this market and will continue reaping the benefits.

Product Differentiator

Globileware has various features that make it different from the competition.

Globileware	Top Competing Products
Connects any client device to any back end applications	Works with specific client devices or back end applications
Delivered as a plug & play appliance device	Delivered as code needed to be programmed into the corporate network
Developed with industry standard technology	Developed with propriety technology

Globileware is one of the first products of this new future. More information about this product can be found at www.globileware.com.

Rohan Hall

Chapter 5

Money and Finances

————

I wish I could say you don't need any money to start a new business, but it wouldn't be true. The question is – how much money you will need and how do you get it?

When I talk about money and financing a business, I like to refer to the Dot comers because I think it was a fascinating point in history. Here you had kids with a vision, technical skills, and no business experience. These kids were given tons of money by adults who had no technical skills, lots of money, and years of business experience. Many of the dot comers ended up filing bankruptcy, as did their investors. Everyone left with a nasty taste in their mouths. Those who didn't file bankruptcy still owe significant amounts of money in capital gain taxes from stocks they capitalized on during that era.

The notable thing about this is: How much money did they *really* need to build that wonderful visionary product? Could they have done it at a fraction of the cost? Well they could and would have if the money hadn't been so easily available. Keep an eye out and you will see a different technology revolution happening. The dot comers will be back, but this time their entry into the market will be significantly more humble.

If at all possible, you should build your own product. While building your product, don't quit your day job. Your biggest assets in this situation are the steady income you receive from your day job and the free time you have (evenings and weekends). You'll save tons of money from this advice alone.

This is important, because there will be areas where you *must* spend money – you won't have a choice. And since the climate has changed, people aren't so willing to invest a fortune for you to develop your ambitions. I believe the coming years will be good for business, but not like the late 90s.

Therefore, much of your financing will come from you and those closest to you. Be aware, however, that each time you take money from someone you give away more control of your business. You also have a responsibility to return the money and profits to those people.

Where am I going with this? I know this is against the grain of what other business type books propose, but I think you should use your own money to finance your business. Depending on your current financial position, this may be hard at first. However, it will keep you honest. You'll be more careful about how you spend your own money, and you'll take fewer risks.

The core value of self-financing your business is control and ownership. Our goal here is to build a profitable business where you can essentially be on vacation for as long as you want while still making money. If you have investors, they won't like the fact that you don't live in the office. They won't understand why you won't follow orders. They'll want to control your life and your business, and you'll end up feeling like an employee again. And worst of all, you really can't quit because you owe them money.

Another reason you shouldn't spend a lot of time trying to get investors at the beginning stages of your business is because fund raising is a time consuming effort and a distraction to you building your business. You will need to create a formal Business Plan and a presentation to sell your ideas to potential investors. It can take weeks to create this. Once it's created, you can spend months finding an investor who'll meet with you. The rejection process can become discouraging and will certainly be a distraction. Your focus at this time should not be on investors; it should be on strategic partners, strategic direction, and product development. Once you've created your Agile business structure and your business is making money, then the doors of investors will be more easily opened. They may actually come looking for you. But by that time, investors may not look as attractive as they seemed in the beginning, unless you need to further expand the business.

To get your business going self finance or informal (friends & family) investors are your best opportunity for financing your dreams.

According to the Global Entrepreneurship Monitor (GEM) project by Babson College, London Business School, and sponsored by the Ewing Marion Kauffman Foundation:

> *It is estimated that informal investors funded 99.962% of all businesses and supplied 91.8% of the total amount invested in the GEM nations; or put differently, fewer than 38 of every 100,000 companies were backed by classic venture capital, which amounted to 8.2% of the total sum invested.*
>
> *Hence, if there was no informal investment there would be virtually no new ventures. In contrast, if there was no venture capital there would be no perceptible drop in the number of new ventures.*
>
> *Across all GEM countries about three in every 100 adults have invested in someone else's business during the last three years. Of those investors, 43.7% report that they invested in a close family member's business, 8.9% in a relative's, 29.2% in a friend or*

neighbor's, 8.9% in a work colleague's, and 9.3% in a stranger's[3]

So how can you self-finance your business? The first point is to understand the financial part of your business. There's no big mystery here. Things cost money, you can budget and make projections, and you can be less ambitious with your initial product. Future projects can be significantly more ambitious, when you've already proven your product and your Agile business structure. One mistake the dot comers made was thinking their initial product should change the world. They also believed initial profits weren't important. They believed running a business with unending losses was okay. I always had a problem with this. I believe your initial product must be profitable and should prove the viability of your network.

In other words, if I build a product, I want to prove the market is interested in buying this product. I also want to know more people will buy this product each month, and I need to make sure everyone who may want this product can have it with a minimum of effort. Also, I want to know I have a profit when I subtract my normal expenses from my revenue. If I'm not profitable during the first few months I should know within reason when I will become profitable.

If I borrow money from investors or the bank, it takes money directly from my pocket each month. It affects the bottom line. I can't just ignore the fact that I owe this money, with the hope of some vague exit strategy. Dot comers built businesses with exit strategies in mind and ignored the basic rule of any business: the business must be profitable or it will fail. I build businesses with a long-term vision of being paid indefinitely from my initial work.

So how much money will you need? Start with one product you can build yourself or one you can afford to buy the

[3] Reynolds, P.D., W.D. Bygrave, and Autio E. 2004. Global Entrepreneurship Monitor: 2003 Executive Report. Babson College, London Business School, and the Kauffman Foundation, page 57, 58

rights to. If you build it yourself, then you have no cost except the time and materials for your initial creation. If you buy it, then negotiate well, get an attorney and make sure you're legally protected to modify/resell this product at will. You can also hire someone to build it for you. If you follow this route, you should get a fixed price and have a contract that specifically states how much time it will take to build and the cost. You might also include penalties if this time schedule isn't met. Most importantly, your contract should clearly state that this is a *work for hire* and upon payment for this work you will own all rights to it. There are common *work for hire* agreements your attorney can draft for you.

Attorneys are expensive however, and can cost thousand of dollars for contracts and agreements. Many of these types of contracts and agreements can cost only a few dollars (often about $10 to $20) if you download them from the internet. The contracts are customized to your needs and can be used in most business situations. You may still want to use an attorney to *review* these documents. The primary difference here is the cost of drafting the documents versus simply reviewing the documents. Attorneys typically charge by the hour, and a good attorney will cost over $200 per hour. It takes hours to create these documents. If you want further modifications to the downloaded documents, simply give the document to an attorney, describe the changes you want, and you'll receive the modifications at a fraction of the cost compared to the attorney drafting the entire document for you.

Don't Quit your Job just Yet

As I stated before, starting a business is risky. If you currently have a source of income, don't give it up until you have enough money from your business to sustain yourself. Sometimes a product may take a few months to reach that point; sometimes it may take a year or two. Sometimes it may not be successful at all. It isn't wise to walk away from your current income situation until you can replace it with something else.

I've been to wealth seminars and read various types of books suggesting you quit your job and pursue your business dreams full time. I find that financially irresponsible. Like anything else, it takes time to build your business. Once you've proven your product and your network, then you'll be able live from your newfound wealth. Until then, be financially wise.

Another reason you should wait before leaving your job is because as long as you have a source of income you'll make better business decisions. You may have a wonderful product, but your timing is simply off. Maybe you're a few years ahead of your time, or perhaps you're a year or two late. Either way, if your product doesn't do as well as you anticipated, you may find yourself desperate. It's a terrible feeling to find out the market doesn't respond to your super idea. If you've already quit your job and you've just spent all your money pursuing this dream, you could experience financial ruin. Even if another opportunity presents itself, you won't be in an emotional or financial position to make good business decisions.

Therefore, keep your day job while you build your business. Think of your day job as a way to finance your current life and your business project. The successful execution of this business project is your true long-term future.

Your Initial Investment

It would be nice to have unlimited funds to build our dream projects. But that won't happen for most of us. Unless

92

you're already wealthy, you probably won't have a lot of money to pursue this dream. Therefore, you should know exactly how much money you can spend on this project.

I don't suggest going into debt to build your initial project. It will be tempting to take out a $20,000 limit credit card to do this if you have good credit. Remember, however, that one day you'll have to repay this loan. I also don't suggest you mortgage your home or incur any other debt. I suggest you take the time to think about your idea and figure out how to make your initial product.

If you do some type of intellectual property product such as a book, a music CD, or computer software, then your cost is virtually nothing. That's the beauty of creating these products; your development cost can be zero.

If you have to spend money to create your product, first analyze how much money you've saved and how much disposable income you have each month. Your budget should be contained to that if possible. This may sound difficult, but one of the things that kill a business the fastest is debt. If you go into debt and have an extra $1000 per month to pay because your new business doesn't generate enough revenue to meet that extra financial obligation, you'll feel an amazing amount of financial stress, fail in your business, and give up on your dream. You may also destroy your credit.

Therefore, keep the initial investment in your business and product at a minimum. By starting off without debt you give yourself a lot of other options.

You initial investment will include:
- Incorporating your business
- Creating/acquiring your initial product
- A computer, for management of your business, possibly creating your product, and conducting research

You will also need money to:
- Manufacture/distribute your product

- Create demand for your product

Things You Should Not Spend Money On
 You will be excited about your business and will want to justify spending money on everything someone pitches to you. That's normal, but here are some expenses you can probably do without:

An Office: With the exception of selling retail or some specific service, you really don't need an office space. It feels nice to have one, but you're simply throwing money away. Start your business from home, if at all possible. Your home address or a P.O. box should be your business address. You can always find a little space on that desk in the corner or the kitchen table to operate your business. You'll find many other ways to spend your money.
 What about if you need to have a meeting with someone? Meet at their office or invite them out to lunch. Try to be creative before you make the decision to sign a lease that will cost you money every month whether or not you're making money.

Employees: Don't hire employees at this stage of your business. Recruit your spouse, children, family members, and friends for *free help*. If you need some professional help, try to find someone that offers this service, and then budget for the extra cost. For example, if you need help preparing documents, don't hire a professional typist or administrative assistant. Find an agency and contract for these services. The difference is long-term cost versus short-term cost. If you hire an employee then you have legal and financial responsibility for this person. Find an individual or group that provides what you need and pay the cost only when you utilize the service.

Stationary: You can create your own documents and business cards using a word processor (MS Word etc.) Since most business use email to transmit documents, your stationary is simply a *"Header"* in your document. Also, since you own the business you can make whatever stationary you want to from your word processor. Ordering stacks of expensive stationary and business cards is a waste of money.

***Attorney Create Original Legal Documents*:** Sample legal documents are available free on the internet. The ones that are not free will probably cost you between $10 and $20. You can download them and use them for your purposes. Verify that the document is not copyright protected. The copyright status will typically be posted on the website where you found the document. Hire an attorney to review and validate these documents before using them. In some situations, you may not be able to find a legal document for your business purposes. On those rare occasions, you might need to have one created. I suggest you write to the best of your knowledge what you would like the document to say. Only then should you see an attorney to translate your document into a legally binding document. If you don't do this, you may find that attorney fees can be a large part of your expenses.

***A Formal Business Plan*:** I can see the MBAs frowning over this one. A business plan is basically your description of your business, product, strategy, financial projections, etc. It's a document someone can read and get a good idea of what you're trying to do. Investors are the people who typically like to see business plans. Business Plans give them insight into what you're thinking, your product ideas, financial projections, market share, and competition. Business Plans are very detailed. If you don't know how to write one however, it can be expensive to have someone do it for you. I don't see the value in this unless you're looking for investors. Since I don't believe in investors (except in specific cases), I think you should save your money. You do, however, need to understand the components of the business plan. This book will discuss those elements. In fact, you can think of this book as your business plan – minus the huge cost of having one written for you.

Money and Accounting

Many business owners (and wealthy individuals) make the mistake of trusting others with their money. It takes knowledge to make money and it takes knowledge to manage your money. Since the beginning of the new millennium, thousands of people have lost money because they trusted money managers, accountants, stockbrokers and a variety of *"experts"* with their money. These experts serve a function. They are there to *assist* with managing your money. You should utilize these professionals and learn from each experience. However YOU should be ultimately responsible for managing your money and your organization.

You don't need to be an accountant or financial advisor, but it's important to understand how money works. You'll need to understand certain basic terms and concepts for building your financial knowledge.

Income (Revenue)

Revenue is the money your business generates, the money you receive from your customers. It's also called income. Without revenue there is no business. Even though it is possible to have a non-revenue generating business, such a business probably won't last long. You should always keep an eye on your revenue. It's an important number and you always want this one to increase.

Expense

Many businesses focus on revenue and forget about expenses. Expenses are no less important than revenue. In fact, expenses should always be considered a percentage of revenue. If this number increases, your revenue should also increase. You should always make every effort to keep your monthly expenses at the lowest level possible.

Net Income (Profit or Loss)

Profit should be top on your list of financial words to focus on. It is the essence of capitalism and the reason you're in business. Profit is what gives you the ability to stop working and start getting rich. Profit is when you have a positive cash flow for your business. It's when you subtract all your expenses from your revenue and there's still money left over.

Income (Profit/Loss) Statement

Your Income Statement tells how well you're doing. You should do this monthly, quarterly and/or yearly. This is a financial statement that tells if your business is profitable. Load your financial transactions into your financial software and it will perform this calculation for you. Your business is profitable if your net income is positive. If net income falls into the negative category, then your business is operating at a loss. If you're operating at a loss then you need to increase your revenue, reduce your expenses, or both.

Sample
Income Statement for March 2005
Income

Product A	$3,000
Product B	$18,500
Product C	$4,500
Total Income	*$26,000*

Expense

Manufacturing	$8,000
Distribution/Fulfillment	$3,000
Sales/Marketing	$4,000
Total Expenses	*$15,000*

Net Income	***$11,000***

You can also calculate net income for specific products. Either way, you're trying to determine how well your company is doing or how well a product is doing.

Liability (Debt)
This is money you owe. It's the same as in your personal life. You need to keep this number as low as possible. The higher this number, the harder you need to work.

Asset
These are things the company owns of value. Based on this business structure, your assets will be your cash, your accounts receivable, your inventory, and the value of your intellectual property.

Stop Working!

Owners Equity

This is the value of your ownership in the business.

Balance Sheet

This is another key financial statement. It shows the value of your assets, liability and equity in the business.

Example
Balance Sheet as of November 16, 2005

Asset

Cash	$5,000
Accounts Receivable	$35,000
Inventory	$55,000
Total Asset	*$95,000*

Liability

ABC Manufacturing	$15,000
XYZ Partners	$12,000
Total Liability	*$27,000*

Owner's Equity	***$68,000***

Cash Basis Accounting

This is what I recommend for new businesses, because its' an easy and simple accounting method. The essence of Cash Basis Accounting is that a transaction isn't considered taxable until it hits your bank account (assuming that all your revenues and expenses flow through your bank account). By using this form of accounting you simply need the transactions from your bank account to form your financial statements and tax records.

A one-minute download from your bank to your financial statement is all you'll need if you use this format.

Accrual Accounting

For larger organizations with employees, long term liabilities, fixed assets (building, machines etc), Cash Basis Accounting is often impractical. Taxable financial transactions for these types of businesses occur at the time of commitment, while Cash Basis Accounting transactions occur at the time the transaction affects your bank account. Accrual Accounting transactions *accrue* (accumulate) over time. Therefore, revenue from a contract must be recorded before you receive the income. Expenses you've committed to but haven't yet paid must also be recorded. These revenue and expense transactions accrue in various accounts in the financial system.

As a small to medium business owner, you should try to use Cash Basis Accounting if possible, because it's simpler and a lot less work than the alternative. Discuss this with your accountant to see what your best option is. Regardless of the accounting method you select, you should learn and understand the financial concepts. Your business may grow to a point that you have no choice but to use Accrual Accounting. Also, you may need to have financial discussions with business partners, your accountant, investors, or your bank. Understanding how different systems work will help you participate more fully in these discussions instead of simply accepting what other people say.

Commonly used terms with Accrual Accounting:

Accounts Payable

Accounts Payable (AP) refers to recording the accumulation and payment of debt. Each time someone sends you a bill you create an accounts payable transaction. When you pay that invoice you create another accounts payable transaction that offsets the original transaction. The core essence of accounts payable is to know what you owe to whom. Consider it a more complicated form of bill payment.

Accounts payable therefore focuses on vendors and the payment of vendors. Each accounts payable system will have a list of all the vendors you pay. Accountants, attorneys, and utility services are common vendors tracked with accounts payable systems.

The three primary types of accounts payable transactions are: you receive an invoice from a vendor; you pay the vendor; and you make an adjustment to a prior transaction.

When transactions are made in the accounts payable system it will eventually flow to the general ledger, which is the official "book" for the company. (See more about the general ledger below).

By using an Accrual Accounting system a company can tell at any moment how much money it owes to each vendor it works with. Large companies tend to have hundreds or even thousands of vendors, so they need a system like this to manage the process.

Cash Basis Accounting doesn't require an accounts payable system, because the IRS doesn't require you to report accrued liability if you use Cash Basis Accounting. Only actual payment of liability need be reported. Therefore, when you use the Cash Basis Accounting you don't need to record bills sent to you by vendors. You only need to record the payment to the vendor. This is why convenient online bill payment provided by your bank is such an asset to your business.

The methods described in this book use strategic partnerships. Your strategic partners will probably use some type of Accural Accounting. By using these partners you reduce the number of vendors you have to work with. You can work on an international scale, utilizing hundreds of vendors; however you may have only a handful of direct vendors yourself. Your business partners will have invested the dollars in software and human resources required to manage these hundreds of vendors. You benefit from their investment without paying the cost.

Accounts Payable/Vendor Network

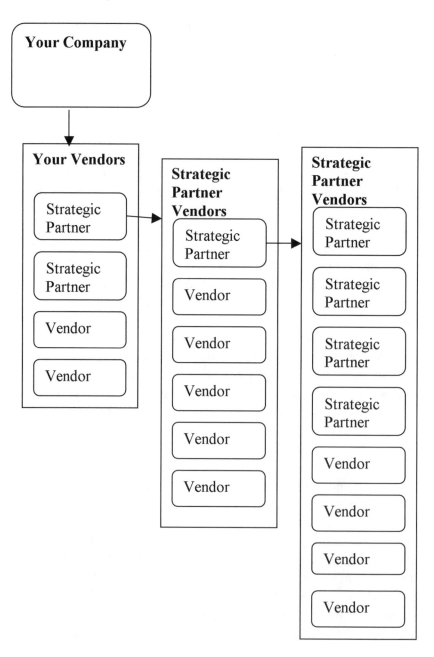

Stop Working!

In this illustration, you use a Cash Basis for Accounting. You have only four vendors. By using strategic partners, you reap the benefits of a multitude of vendors, but have no responsibility to manage or track any of these transactions. You only have to track payments made to your four direct vendors.

Accounts Receivable

Accounts Receivable refers to recording invoices sent to customers and funds received from customers. With Accrual Accounting, a financial transaction must occur each time a customer is invoiced for products or services. This financial transaction is a record showing the date the customer was invoiced, the amount, and for what reason. Each time the company receives funds from the customer, another transaction occurs for the funds received. The core value of an accounts receivable system is to track money owed to the company and payments received by the company.

Accounts Receivable is the flip side of accounts payable. It can be confusing at first, because similar words are used to describe both functions. One of the best ways to remember the difference is that accounts *payable* is bill *payment* and accounts *receivable* is cash *receipts*.

Accounts receivable focuses on customers. An accounts receivable system will include a list of all customers with whom you conduct business. The system will track how much money each customer owes you and how much they've paid. When customers don't pay their bills, various reports are run from the accounts receivable system. These reports are used by the credit and collections department – the people who send out nasty letters or call to remind you of your past due account.

Accounts receivable systems also keep historic information. When companies have to determine your credit ratings, they may look at historic data regarding your payment history with them. This data is stored in the company's accounts receivable system.

Transactions processed (posted) in the accounts receivable system will eventually migrate to the General Ledger system (see below).

By using Accrual Basis Accounting, a company can tell at any given moment all its customers and the amount of money each customer owes. The company can also retrieve payment histories and track various payment trends. Companies can have hundreds or thousands of customers they do business with on a regular basis, and the accounts receivable process helps them manage this vast number of customers.

When you use Cash Basis Accounting you only need to record the receipt of funds. Basically, recording each deposit or credit to your bank account is the only tax requirement.

By using strategic partners you exponentially increase your customer base without increasing the number of customers you manage. Your strategic partner will invest the dollars required to track each customer. Your relationship with them will allow you to use this technology without extra cost.

Accounts Receivable/Customer Network

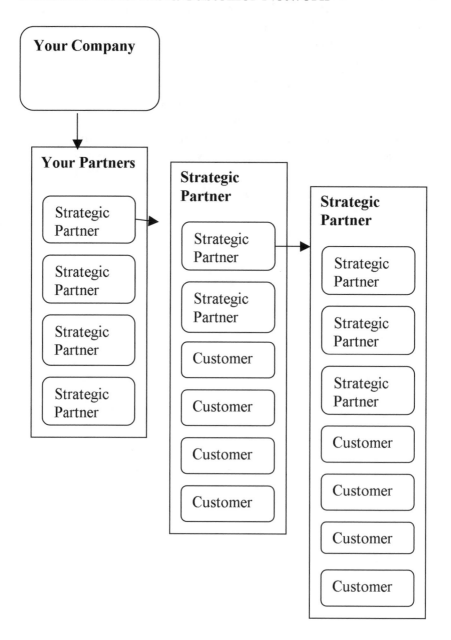

Stop Working!

In this illustration you use strategic partners with access to a massive customer network. These partners are often distributors and retailers with established customer networks. Their networks may include many other networks and span the entire globe. By using distributors and retailers, you never need to track a single customer, because they'll track the customers for you. You don't need complex accounts receivable systems; your partners have already made that investment. You don't need to build a network of customers; your partners already have a network. Your primary duty will be to find the best partners, create the right business deals, and let them do all the work. They will expose your products to their vast network and manage all customer relationships, invoicing and receipts, and customer services. Your partners are paid a percentage of sales; therefore it's hard for you not to be profitable. It's up to you to understand the money.

By using strategic partners your products can have an immediate global exposure with an established global sales team, and you don't have to do any work.

In this scenario, you have no direct customers, no invoices to send, and no customer relationships. Yet you still receive a sizable check or direct deposit from your distributors and retailers who sell your products.

General Ledger

A General Ledger is the *book* of original entry. It's your legal financial record. All financial transactions for an organization eventually end up in the General Ledger. This includes accounts payable, accounts receivable, purchasing, inventory etc. If you're audited by the IRS or by an audit firm, the first thing they'll ask to see is your General Ledger.

The financial statements mentioned above, plus a Balance Sheet and Income Statement are created from data in your General Ledger. Therefore, it's the common element for all financial systems and the most important piece.

Both Cash Basis Accounting and Accrual Accounting use a General Ledger. By using a Cash Basis for accounting you avoid the complexities of other accounting systems. You go straight to the end result, which is to have good, accurate, manageable books you can use to run your company.

Show Me the Money

Money & Finance
========

Both vConcepts and Eye Contact Media use Cash Basis Accounting from an off-the-shelf accounting package. Transactions from both companies are downloaded from our bank to the financial software. The transactions are validated and arranged in categories, such as meals and entertainment, office expenses, book sales etc.

Neither company has any debt. A zero debt situation allows us to be significantly more selective about our projects. We choose projects that are fun, interesting, and profitable and where we can make a great contribution to our clients or the project itself.

I won't say I'll never have debt, but since I've been deep under personal debt before, I'd need an incredible reason to do it again.

All my business transactions flow through my business accounts. I use my check card for everything, unless I write a business check. My book of record stems from my bank statements. All transactions are therefore easily traceable, which reduces my risks of accounting errors.

I haven't quit my job yet as CEO of vConcepts, Inc and Eye Contact Media. I still provide services as an ERP consultant to my clients. I have great clients and enjoy what I do. I like building technology, and I enjoy building companies. For many that's work, but for me it's fun. It's rewarding because I choose to do it instead of having to do it.

The System is Eye Contact Media's first product. It requires no attention. I log on to check status reports occasionally, but nothing else. My distributors are busy selling my products to retailers. The retailers are busy selling my products to end customers. We run various marketing and promotion efforts to create demand for our products. I spend most of my time thinking strategically about new markets to get into and new products to release via my Agile business structure.

Both The System and Globileware are generating revenues without my intervention. I will continue adding more products to this revenue stream, and this book is one of those products. Even if one product becomes less successful over time, others will be there to continue generating cash flow.

Chapter 6

Management Tips

The Effective Executive

I've been privileged to work with various types of executives. Some have been very effective, while others were not.

One would assume that the most effective executives work around the clock and make sure they squeeze every ounce of productivity from their employees. I've found the opposite is true: the most effective executives I know rarely work late, take regular vacations, and freely delegate responsibility to others in their organization. And these executives seem happy.

Effective executives are a rare find and an absolute pleasure to work with. Over the span of my 20-year career in business I've been privileged to meet a variety of executives on a business and personal level. With each opportunity, I've been able to inquire about their core values. What makes someone rise to the top while others fail? What are the essential ingredients required to manage a business? Here are some of the things I learned:

Know your business and your products

Effective executives know their products and their business. If you ever want to test this, just ask about their top product, the demographics of their best customers, and the current sales trends for that product market. They make every effort to keep abreast of their product and what's happening in the market.

Effective executives know their business. They understand their managers and employees, the company's strength and weaknesses, and the opportunities and failures of the company. They also know their competitors. They understand the primary technology the company uses, their critical business processes, and opportunities for improvement.

Hire the Best and Delegate Responsibility

Effective executives always seek and hire the best employees they can find. They realize that the sum effort of these individuals is a reflection of their organization. By hiring the best they're able to delegate critical business functions, which frees them to focus on the organization's strategic vision.

Never be a part of any core operational process

Effective executives are never a core part of any operational business process. They assign this responsibility to employees, after placing checks and balances to ensure the successful completion and validation of each task. An effective executive will review the completion of tasks, but won't be part of the business process required to complete the task.

Stop Working!

Your Two Jobs

As a self-employed individual, you will have the full responsibility of your organization. You can choose to fill every role yourself, or you can follow the path of this book. I strongly suggest you have only two jobs:

- Effective Executive
- Artist

Be an Effective Executive

As an Effective executive you must first learn all the principles in this book. The execution of this knowledge will make you rich.

You must understand your product and your business. Whatever product you decide to make, you should be convinced it's something the market needs. You should learn everything about your product and the market. Most of this information is free on the Internet today. You should also check with bookstores for information on these products. I like online bookstores because of convenience and discount prices. I also like brick and mortar bookstores because I can go inside, touch the book, read the materials, and compare with other books before I buy. You should also check magazine racks, attend seminars, and talk to people. Leave no stone unturned to find information about your product and your market.

You must delegate everything except control of your money. No one has access to my bank account except for direct deposit. My wife and I review our own business bank accounts and financial records. All other business processes should be delegated or outsourced. By using this method you delegate routine business tasks to professionals who are staffed and equipped to perform the required duties. By choosing to perform these duties yourself, you tie yourself to long working hours, costly processes, and ineffective business practices.

Outsourcing is a big, nasty word today in American business. When I say outsource, I don't mean send your core operational processes to a foreign country to people who are cheap and incompetent. By outsourcing, I mean finding strategic partners in whom you have the highest level of confidence. A variety of business partners in your country would love to partner with you and have your business. They are capable, competent, and inexpensive. Doing the same work yourself could be a financial and operational nightmare. Find more than one trusted partner that you can utilize for these tasks. If there's an issue with one partner, you should be able to switch to the other with little or no effort.

As you go through the process of deciding who your strategic partners are, you must always consider the employees of your partner firm to be your employees. Your standards should be as high or higher than if you actually hired them yourself. They represent your company in the way they build your product, market your product, distribute your product, and the other business functions they provide for you.

You must not be a part of any core business process. We explore various business processes in this book and it's important for you to understand them. Once you identify the ones that are needed for your business, you should find competent strategic partners to perform those duties. Stay out of their way while they perform the duties. If you're able to do this with all your processes, the business will run efficiently whether you're in town or on vacation. It won't matter. Each strategic partner will act independently, but will be integrated. You become a hindrance and a liability to your business if you insert yourself into the flow of these integrated processes.

Manage your business, don't run your business. When you *run* your business you are at the wheel everyday. You are trying to do all the business processes needed to keep your business afloat. You are always working hard and are always tired. You are too busy working hard and not busy enough getting rich. When you *manage* a business, you review key reports, ensure resources are available to those who need them, and plan and direct the business toward your vision. You should manage your business daily instead of trying to run it. At any given time you should know key indicators for sales, inventory, cash etc through web access from your strategic partners. It only takes a few minutes per day to manage your business, but it's required.

I manage my business from anywhere in the world. I don't even use a laptop anymore. Internet cafes are everywhere we travel. If I'm in a foreign country I can walk into an Internet café and log onto my bank accounts, distributor accounts, and retailer's accounts. I take a few minutes to check my bank balance, level of inventory, current product demand, and sales. I also check my corporate email online via POP mail. It takes only a few minutes each day to manage my business. Because of my strategic partnerships and their technology and business processes, my business runs itself.

You should never try to do everything yourself. You need to find other businesses to partner with. Hundreds of thousands of businesses are waiting to do your work for you. There's a cost, but the cost is often less than if you performed the tasks yourself. People who try to do all the business processes themselves become slaves of their own companies. They can't take vacations, they have no free time, they become stressed, and their company never expands or grows. Eventually, they become disillusioned and confused. They start wishing for a nice comfortable job at someone else's company. They think it's easier to make someone else rich than to make themselves rich.

Finding the right partners can be difficult and time consuming. It takes a lot of research. This is where the investment in your computer becomes even more important. Everything you want can be found on the Internet. I'm convinced of it. I have partners all over the world I've never met and will never meet. These relationships are a result of extensive Internet research. I have the greatest confidence in them because I did my research before creating these partnerships.

Set Goals

Tons of books have been written about goals. I won't beat this subject to death, but a couple things are worth mentioning:

Set a five- year goal – I think failure is easily found in short term goals. You'll be amazed at what you can do in five years and how fast the time will pass. I always have five year goals, and these goals read like a fantasy, because I think of the ideal life I'd like to have. These are things that are worth working for. If you're poor, working on a five year goal to become wealthy is worth working at. If you're overweight or obese then a goal to finish a marathon and to be in ideal physical shape are goals worth working for. Five-year goals should be amazing and fantastic.

At 30 years old I set a few five-year goals. One was to travel to two countries per year. I'd never done any traveling at that time and wanted to see the world. I had little money and could barely imagine going to a different country every year. Two countries per year seemed extreme, but I really wanted to do it. It was worth working for. Three years after setting that goal I had visited about 20 countries.

Another goal I had was financial. I wanted to have enough net worth *"to retire and work at McDonalds if I wanted to while living a comfortable lifestyle."* On the fourth year I had surpassed this financial goal. In fact, I more than doubled my income every year for the first three years after I set that goal.

I also had personal goals with family and relationships. I met and surpassed all these goals.

Set one-year goals – I feel like I could die every time I hear someone set a new year's resolution. These are pie in the sky dreams people set because they feel guilty about the failures in

116

their lives. These resolutions often fail because they aren't part of a bigger picture. Most new years resolutions are forgotten a month after they're made.

Set one-year goals every year. I set them at the beginning of the year. These aren't New Year's resolutions – they're goals I can achieve for that year, and they always tie into my five-year goals. At the end of every year I review my *written* goals for the past 12 months and check them off my list. It's a great feeling of accomplishment to check these things off the list.

I use the end of every year (December or January) to reflect on the year just completed. I review the things I did right and what I did wrong. I check off the things I accomplished and question the things I didn't accomplish. I then make a new list for the new year.

In doing this I ask myself a variety of questions. What else can I do to achieve my five-year plan? What can I do better or more efficiently?

Balanced Goals – It's great to say *I want to be rich*. I think money is a wonderful thing. It's also great to say *I want to be happy*. I think happiness is the reason for life. My personal phrase is, *Happiness is next to Godliness.* But the truth is, I don't want to be poor and happy or rich and miserable. I want a balanced life. Because of this, all my five-year goals must fall under the following categories from a childhood song:

- Happy
- Healthy
- Wealthy
- Wise

The combination of these things is what I call my balance. These are my core values and all my goals must fall within them. As I set my goals each year, I ask myself: Does this goal fall within one of these values?

Happy –Five-year goals for happiness might include:

117

- Strong relationships with each member of my family
- The best possible relationship with my wife
- Enjoy every moment possible with my children
- Enjoy my time as I choose
- Visit at least two countries on each continent
- Find new ways to contribute to the lives of others

Healthy –Five-year goals for being healthy might include:

- Being in the best physical condition possible
- Running five miles every day
- Complete a marathon
- Defeat any health problems
- Care more about myself and my decisions

Wealthy –Five-year goals for wealth might include:

- To retire (based on your definition of retirement)
- Put my child through college
- Build a multinational multi-million dollar business
- Have a positive cash flow of $250,000 per year and a net worth of $2 million

Wise –Five-year goals for wisdom might include:

- Go back to college and finally complete that degree
- Obtain a Ph.D.
- Learn to speak French and spend a summer in France
- Be the best and most knowledgeable person in my field
- Learn from the elders – while there's time

You should have at least two or three items, but no more than five in each category. Include only things that are most important to you; things you want to work toward every day for the next five years. You should be able to visualize your life with these goals accomplished – and it should make you smile. You must have some level of passion for each goal.

Each goal must also be specific. The five-year goal may be a little vague but not too vague. The one-year goal must be specific. Weekly and daily goals must be specific tasks. The more specific your goals are, the better your chance of achieving them. A goal of "being rich" isn't really a goal – it's more like a dream or a wish. What is rich? It's different to everyone and it will change as you make more money. A better goal would be a net worth of one million dollars, or a business that yields a residual net cash flow of $500,000 per year.

If your goal is "to be rich," you may have one million dollars in your account and still not feel you've achieved your goal. In that case, you may feel like a failure. Many people today with a large net worth or large incomes believe they've failed because they don't have a concrete definition of success. You don't want to be one of these people.

Also, by writing your goals you give life to this mission. Over the years you will review the goals. When you achieve them, what once seemed a fantasy will give you the greatest level of satisfaction regarding what you can achieve. You will feel successful! Your confidence and self-esteem will benefit from this newfound success. You will create new dreams and your *next* five-year goals will be even more incredible.

I believe financial success without personal success creates a losing situation. Everyone knows people with material goods who can't seem to find happiness or balance in their lives. We see it often with high profile divorces in Hollywood, and with people who seem to have everything and still commit suicide.

To be an Effective Executive, I believe you will need to be a balanced individual. You can have it all, but you need to plan for it.

You must have a vision for yourself and your company five years from today – and you will need to be obsessive about achieving these goals.

Be an Obsessive Compulsive Manager

Setting goals and achieving them are two different things. I tend to be pretty good at both – not because I'm super smart, but because of certain habits of mine. I consider myself an obsessive-compulsive manager. If you've ever taken a psychology class you probably know something about obsessive compulsive disorder. If not, here's the official definition from the National Institute of Mental Health:

> *Obsessive-Compulsive Disorder, OCD, is an anxiety disorder and is characterized by recurrent, unwanted thoughts (obsessions) and/or repetitive behaviors (compulsions). Repetitive behaviors such as hand washing, counting, checking, or cleaning are often performed with the hope of preventing obsessive thoughts or making them go away. Performing these so-called "rituals," however, provides only temporary relief, and not performing them markedly increases anxiety.[4]*

In psychological terms, to be obsessive/compulsive is a bad thing. I don't want you to have a psychological problem but I believe that applying some of these characteristics to your goals can be a good thing. Let me explain what I mean. We can attain success in almost any area based on the level of commitment and *consistent* effort we expend toward a specific goal. In fact, I consider my personal success formula to be:

Success Formula = Goals + Achieve task EVERY DAY toward that goal

Therefore, if you have a goal to build a business with gross revenues of two million dollars within two years, you need to do something toward that goal EVERY DAY until you achieve it. Working on your business only once a week means you'll take at least seven times as long to achieve your goal.

I am obsessive-compulsive because every single day I do something toward achieving my goals. Every day I must ask

[4] *Source (http://www.nimh.nih.gov/)*

myself at least three key questions that support the success of this goal. Every day I must achieve something toward these ultimate goals. The questions I ask are different and the tasks that I achieve are different, but they always focus on answering the primary question: *what can I do today toward achieving this specific goal?*

Imagine if every day you make a specific effort toward your goal of building your successful business. In seven days you'll achieve at least seven tasks. Most days you'll be able to achieve multiple tasks. I typically perform at least three tasks per day, so in seven days I've **completed** 21 steps toward my goals. In one year I typically achieve at least 1,008 tasks towards my five-year plan.

In five years of doing specific things towards my goals I achieve at least 5,040 separate tasks. Now you see why I always reach my goals. This simple formula has never failed me.

	Per week	Per Month	Per Year	5 Years
1 task per week	1	4	48	240
1 task per day	7	28	336	1,680
3 tasks per day	21	84	1,008	5,040
5 tasks per day	35	140	1,680	8,400

A task is what most people call a goal for the day. It could be an assignment to research strategic partners that would manufacture my product; send emails to these contacts; challenge myself with more creative ways to spend money and time more wisely; or finding new ways to market my products. Working on these tasks can take minutes or hours, depending on how much available time you have. You're in complete control of this.

A task can be questions you ask yourself. Even when I go skiing, I'm obsessive about my goals. Down the slope I ask myself questions, such as "Do we have our book in every country we want it to be? How can we reach other markets? Do we have the best partners today to help us achieve our goals? What else can we do to improve sales or increase efficiency? What else can I do to increase demand? What else can I do today toward this goal?"

Every day I *complete* at least two or three tasks toward achieving my goals. Every day! That may not seem like a lot, but how many things did you do today toward your goal of getting rich?

My available time determines how much I do on any given day, but doing at least one thing each day quickly becomes a positive habit. This is what I call my success habit. Over your lifetime you've developed the habit of taking a shower, combing your hair, and brushing your teeth every day. You don't think about these tasks, you just do them. When you don't do it you feel weird (and dirty).

When you make a habit of working toward your goals every day you become obsessive about your goals and compulsive with your daily tasks.

Daily Tasks and Self Validation

I always keep a notebook and a pen with me wherever I go. You never know when a good idea will hit you. I write these ideas in my notebook and check them off when I'm done. I make task lists weekly and check them off daily when I'm done. I add tasks to my list as I think of them. I learned this from my mother. When you write something, it becomes real. When you check it off, you know you've achieved something. Check it off and pat yourself on the back – this is called self-validation. As a manager you won't always have someone to validate your achievements, so you need to do it yourself. My mother would say, "*I give you permission to validate yourself for all your achievements. You should never wait for someone else to pat you on the back.*"

Stop Working!

Be an Artist

Your second job will be an artist. As an artist you create products for your company. You don't have to physically create the product yourself, but you do need the vision to determine what the product will be. Otherwise, how will you communicate with the person who does the actual development?

Many businesses start with an idea for a product or service, perhaps a vision of something that can be offered to fill a need in the current or future market. Artists often don't know how to translate this vision into a successful business enterprise. It's my vision that this book will help artists with this process.

Artists today express themselves in a variety of ways. Look around: everything you see was created by an artist, a visionary. Someone designed the computer keyboard I use to type this book. Someone wrote the software that checks my spelling. Someone invented the snow tires that are on my car. Someone created the songs I listen to every day. Someone created the laces in my shoes. Someone created the coffee mug I drink from everyday. Each of these people are artists who created a product from an idea. They were probably paid for this work, but did they reap any profit from their creativity?

If you're reading this book, you're probably an artist. I was excited only a few years ago during the dotcom revolution when technology artists were popping up everywhere. Some of these people were able to convert their ideas and talents to successful businesses. But most however weren't so fortunate – they started companies that failed over time. They failed not because of a bad idea, but because they had bad business skills.

One value of this book is that as an artist you can focus on what you really enjoy doing and express your creativity. This process encourages you to build the best products you can while using technology and partners to run the business. Once your business structure has been created you spend only a few minutes managing your business and as much time as you wish being an artist.

Why only two jobs?

Being an effective executive and being an artist are the two most important jobs in your organization, and the areas where you add the most value. No one will manage your company as passionately as you will. No one has the vision you do about your business. If the company fails, you're the one who'll suffer the greatest financial and emotional loss. As an artist, no one is more intimately connected to your product. Your product and your company evolved from your heart.

All other roles in the company are important, but they don't require the same passion – they simply require competence. If the person or partner isn't competent, then replace them. This is why the quality of research you do before establishing strategic relationships is very important. Take all the time you need for due diligence with your research.

Research, Research, Research

Not every business makes a good strategic partner. Research, research, research each step of this process. The difference between a good partner and a bad one could cost you a fortune. As we go through the book I'll help you identify certain questions you should ask prospective strategic partners. It's important that you pick the best one available, and backup partners as well.

Show Me the Money

Management Tips

========

Eye Contact Media, Inc. (www.eyecontactmedia.com)

Manager

Since building our Agile business structure, I've spent less than an hour per day managing this business. There's really nothing to do. All my strategic partners do all the work. I check a variety of online reports daily, usually at the beginning of the day. I know what our daily sales are; I know our best markets; I am aware of product demand and inventory levels. I understand all the business processes my partners are using to manufacture, distribute, and sell our product but I've removed myself from being a part of any of those tasks. My greatest value as a manager is thinking strategically about where I'd like to take this company in the future and how to get there. Through research I've already identified different partners with the access required to take me to this next level.

This freedom is the result of setting clear goals and completing multiple tasks daily. Both my wife and I spent a significant amount of time during the first year of the business achieving our goals. The goal for the first year was to build and test our Agile business structure and have a global presence. We also had a variety of other goals that supported our 5-year plan. Our goals fall into the categories of happy, healthy, wealthy, and wise. We've both committed to having a balanced life as we pursue this and other goals.

Year two of this business is easier because we met the goals of year one. To meet the goals of year one took significantly more work and effort than year two. We spent hours every day working on strategic planning and relationships. A lot of the work involved research and follow up. We spent countless hours on the Internet, researching companies that could be potential strategic partners for manufacturing, distribution, marketing and other functions.

Along with our research, we also did follow up emails and phone calls. It was sometimes difficult to schedule meetings, because I wasn't readily available, since I had to continue working with clients from my other business. By far, my wife did most of the research and communication, while I provided strategic direction, attended meetings, and made the final product and business decisions.

After a few months we'd tested and selected some good partners and had negotiated some excellent deals. We had our agile structure up and tested within a few months. We spend the rest of year one optimizing our product and our processes. We also used the time for monitoring and trend analysis, trying to learn when, how, why, and where customers were buying our products. We used that information in the marketing campaign we initiated toward the end of year one.

Year two is primarily about product expansion, as we add a variety of products to our catalog. We'll also include additional marketing to increase awareness and demand for our products and business.

Year three will focus on market expansion. The world is a large place and we'd like everyone who'd benefit from our products to have the opportunity to buy them, no matter where they live or what language they speak. We will also focus on greater market awareness.

The ultimate goal of Eye Contact Media is to generate unlimited residual income. We've already achieved that to some level. We believe we also have an opportunity to help other people via this forum – and that's one of our goals. All our products will have that component as an integral part of our offering. This lends itself to our need for balance as a part of our goals. Wealth alone isn't enough, although it's an important piece of our formula for balance and fulfillment.

Artist

As an artist I spend as much time as I can working on new products – including the book you're reading. When this book is introduced into our Agile network, I'll once again have a lot of free time. I enjoy writing, so I really don't think of it as working. It's fun! Plus, I enjoy it because I like the idea of helping other people to become rich and escape from the corporate rat race.

vConcepts

Manager

vConcepts is both a consulting organization and a products organization.

As a consulting organization I provide clients with personal hands on attention. I negotiate projects, help build project plans, manage employees and project groups, provide business and technical training, and help resolve a variety of business and technical issues.

As a manager it's difficult to get away from some of these responsibilities. Actually, I haven't made a significant effort to take myself out of this picture, because I enjoy doing these things. They are the core of our business and our clients appreciate this personal attention.

As a products organization, Globileware is licensed to our very competent strategic partners. They have an expansive global sales and technology network and are responsible for the various business processes required to manufacture, market, distribute, and sell the Globileware product. I have removed myself for these daily business processes.

However, I am engaged in the long-term strategic development of the product and the organization. The product will continue to be enhanced to incorporate a variety of new and emerging technologies. I will continue to be part of this process.

Artist

I developed Globileware with a team of highly skilled technologists, and the product is something we're all proud of. It's one of the best on the market and delivers in a way no other product does today. We intend to continue expanding the product's functionality. However, continued development of the application will be done by our partners. Even though I believe I offer value to the continued design and focus of the technology, I don't believe writing the computer code required for the continued growth of the technology is the best way to maximize my time.

By separating myself from this task, I have a lot more time to focus on developing the company, designing other products, or simply stop working if I choose to.

Chapter 7

Manufacturing

———

Manufacturing is reproducing your product for public consumption. After you design your product and create a prototype, you need a way to mass product this product. The process of reproducing your product is referred to as manufacturing.

As a small business owner you really can't afford to take on this business function. The cost of people, equipment, tools and technology required to manufacture most products would be astronomical. There are also various requirements and regulations for manufactured products. This business function should certainly be passed on to a business partner with the resources and expertise to manufacture your product. Additionally as you grow, you'll realize that by having strategic partners perform the manufacturing function you will give yourself unlimited capacity.

People

Even though most state of the art manufacturing facilities are well equipped with automation, there is always the need for people to operate and manage this automation. The people required will be a combination of skilled and unskilled workers. Skilled workers may be involved in tasks such as production planning and operating various types of automated equipment. Unskilled workers may perform tasks such as assembly of the product and clean up.

Prototype

A confusion that new business owner may make is to confuse manufacturing with prototyping. Prototyping is the creation of your initial product. You can create the prototype yourself or have someone create it for you. When you manufacture, you are essentially copying your prototype so you can sell it to the public.

Capacity

Capacity is a common term in manufacturing plants and refers to the ability to produce your goods. As a small business, your capacity to manufacture your own goods would be limited if you did it yourself. Initially you might be able to keep up with the demand for your product, but growth would quickly outreach your capacity. By teaming up with one or more manufacturing partners you give yourself virtually unlimited capacity. If one partner maxes out on their capacity to product your product, you can simply add another partner. Production continues, but now you have doubled your capacity without the need for new equipment or resources.

Quality

You always want to have the best quality for your product. To manufacture your own product requires a lot of skill and commitment. Do you have the skills to do this while expanding your business? I believe in putting the experts to work. Find a partner that produces high quality products in your market and engage them in doing the same for you. Your customers won't know who manufactures the product. They'll assume you did it at your manufacturing plant. Insist on the highest quality from your partners. If they don't perform, then replace them with someone who meets your standards.

Price

As a small business owner, it isn't cost efficient to manufacture your own products; you'll end up buried in debt before you make your first dollar. You'll face costs for buildings, equipment, utilities, people, and tools. You may also have various regulatory fees with local agencies to establish your manufacturing plant. You need to make sure you know the manufacturing standards for your products and meet them. The cost will become prohibitive. Use a manufacturing partner who can give you the exact price per product, calculated as a percentage of your revenue from the product. You only pay for what's manufactured and you only manufacture what you can afford. As sales increase, you can manufacture more because you'll be able to afford it. The eventual sale of your inventory will recover all your manufacturing costs. However, if you were to do it yourself you might never recover all your overhead and initial setup costs. Also, make sure you understand the minimum and maximum amount required for a manufacturing order.

Manufacturing Partners

I suggest you spend a lot of time researching potential partners. Most of this information can be found on the Internet.

Find someone who does this for your specific market instead of using a generalist.

Once you've done research and you're comfortable with your knowledge of the options, you should call everyone you're considering. This isn't a waste of time, because you'll gain information with each encounter. Write a list of questions about the company, their procedures, equipment, business process, cost, delivery time, insurance etc. You want to know everything possible. You're choosing a partner who'll become an important part of your business and your success.

You should also ask about other relationships they have. Do they have the capacity to meet the demand? If not, do they have other partners who will help them to meet this demand? Be aware of the packages they try to sell you. Try not to make any commitments until you've interviewed all the candidates. If at all possible, try to obtain a sample of their work. Do they have clients you may know of? Get references and check them.

Once you've finished the interviews and you feel you have the partner you want to work with, do the numbers again. Work with a spreadsheet and list all the charges. Make sure you specifically ask them to detail all their charges on paper. Are there monthly charges? Do they charge per item? When are these charges payable? How will you pay? If there are fixed overhead charges, you'll calculate it as a per item charge against your product price.

Cost Calculations

You should always keep an eye on your cost of doing business. Before finalizing a relationship, you should be clear about all the costs involved in building, distributing, and selling your product. I'll use a scenario through the rest of the book to show you one way you can look at your cost foundation. I'll list the primary operational revenue and expenses you'll need to keep an eye on.

The scenario assumes you designed and prototyped your own product. You have only one product. You use partners to

manufacture, distribute, market, and sell your product. In the
first year of business you manufacture and sell 5000 items.
That's about 416 items per month on average. The retail price
for your product is $39.99. You should adjust these numbers to
your own needs.

Looking at the primary costs that go into this should help
guide your thinking as you consider the financial management of
your Agile business.

Operational Revenue/Expense Worksheet

	5000 Items	Per Item	% of Sales
Revenue			
Gross Sales	$199,950.00	$39.99	
Manufacturing			
Manufacture Product	$3,750.00	$0.75	1.88%

Based on the above example, it will cost $3,750 to
manufacture 5000 of your items. The cost for each item is 75
cents. You can't possibly sell the product for less than 75 cents
and expect to stay in business very long. There will be other
costs involved and we'll talk about them in future chapters.
However, you have to create a chart like this for each cost you
have in your business. You need to define each cost as a cost per
item and then make the cost a percentage of your revenue.

When you decide to manufacture your item, you should
decide how many items you need to manufacture initially.
There's usually a minimum required by the manufacturer, and
you'll probably receive a discount for larger quantities. You have
to weigh the discount versus the total cost of manufacturing your
item. To manufacture 5000 items might cost 75 cents per item,
while manufacturing 300 items would cost $1.50 per item.

Manufacturing discounts

	Cost	Cost per Item
Manufacture 5000 items	$3,750.00	$0.75
Manufacture 300 items	$525.00	$1.75

Even though you may have a lower cost per item to manufacture 5000 items, you might choose to manufacture only 300 items for your initial product introduction. This lowers your overall cost and gives you an opportunity to test the market need for your product.

You may also want to make adjustments to your product before you do a larger second manufacturing order. Keep these options in mind as you approach this situation.

Offshore Partners

A phrase called *offshoring* is used synonymously with *outsourcing* in current politics. **Offshoring** is using offshore partners, and it's viewed as the moving of jobs from one's country overseas. This is seen as a cheap source of labor that threatens local economies. **Outsourcing** is using partners both domestic and international.

The true value of offshoring is the acquisition of high value partners overseas. A product that may take 75 cents to manufacture, like the example above, may only cost 30 cents in a foreign country. The savings can be 50% of your cost or greater. Mega organizations find savings like that too tempting to resist, therefore most of them now utilize some sort of offshoring. The old saying *a dollar saved is a dollar earned* come into play here.

One has to look at the overall cost of offshoring before making a decision about its financial value. A variety of hidden costs can be incurred, such as rework because the product doesn't meet standards; longer lead time because the product has to be shipped back to your country; customer dissatisfaction because of unqualified resources; shipping costs; and piracy because the offshore country doesn't have laws that protect intellectual rights and property. These are all things you should consider when selecting an offshore partner.

Also consider the fact that Mega Organizations using offshore resources gain a potential financial edge. They may be able to present their product at a significant discount to yours if their expected cost savings is realized.

As a business owner you will have to take all these factors into consideration before deciding if you want offshore partners to manufacture your products.

Purchasing

Your manufacturing partner will have established relationships with vendors, allowing them to purchase materials to manufacture your product at a discounted price. This discounted materials cost may make the difference in what it cost you to manufacture your product. For example, it could cost you $4 to manufacture your product from one manufacturing partner while it could cost you $2 for the same work from another partner. Even though that may not seem like a large difference, the difference is twice the cost - which could reduce your profit by half. Please note the cost/profit difference below:

Partner	Units	Cost / Unit	Cost	Retail Cost/ Unit	Retail	Profit
Partner A	100,000	$2	$200,00	$6	$600,00	$400,00
Partner B	100,000	$4	$400,00	$6	$600,00	$200,00

By selecting Partner A, you would double your profits and put an additional $200,000 in your pocket.

Before selecting your manufacturing partner, you should conduct an extensive search of potential partners. Large manufacturing partners will have lower costs to purchase goods, because they can purchase in large quantities from their vendors. Their ability to purchase raw materials at a low cost and pass these cost savings on to you is a valuable asset. To purchase the raw materials yourself would be even more expensive. Where your partner may purchase high quality supplies at a wholesale price, you may only be able to purchase at a retail price (or wholesale with a smaller discount).

Show Me the Money

Manufacturing
=======

Eye Contact Media, Inc. (www.eyecontactmedia.com)
Eye Contact Media is an American company that focuses on the global market. We are committed to producing the highest quality products available for our customers. Our first product was manufactured in the United States. This isn't done because of protectionism – it's because our manufacturing partner offered the highest quality for the lowest cost. We expect to have a combination of US manufacturing partners as well as offshore partners in the future. It's practical from a cost point of view, but also since we are selling products in other countries, it may be logistically practical to manufacture in some of those countries as well. Our global network is constantly expanding as we try to reach more people all over the world we are constantly on the lookout for more strategic partners to do business with. Through these manufacturing relationship we also have access to an international distribution network. The total value of this relationship is a part of our strategic plan for the continued globalization of our products and our organization.

vConcepts, Inc. (www.vconceptsinc.com)

vConcepts is also an American company. Our clients are primarily multi-national organizations located in a variety of countries. We've worked with these clients in the United States as well as in their local countries to develop a variety of technologies.

All work for our Globileware product, including development, design and testing was done in the United States. Additional testing for the product was also performed in Europe and Asia to verify a variety of communication protocols the application takes advantage of.

We utilize several partners in different regions of the world to sell and distribute this product, but manufacturing is done in the United States.

Rohan Hall

Chapter 8

Distribution

———————

      Distribution is one of the most complex areas in any business and companies couldn't function without it. Although distribution is the core of a business, it's often one of the most ignored areas.

      Distribution relies on a general process called Supply Chain Management (SCM) and various technologies that are used to facilitate the processes. ERP technologies include SCM modules as a part of the application. It integrates SCM with your Manufacturing and Financial Management processes. In fact, you can think of Distribution as the link between the Financial Management and Manufacturing processes. Please note the following illustration:

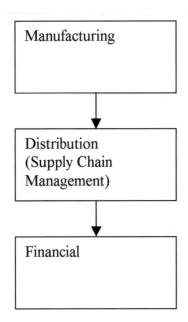

Stop Working!

Distribution has various components that are critical to linking customers, partners, suppliers and your products. The primary business processes involved are: Purchasing, Order Management, and Inventory Management. The following shows a more detailed relationship between distribution, financial, and manufacturing business processes.

Manufacturing, Distribution, Financial Business Processes

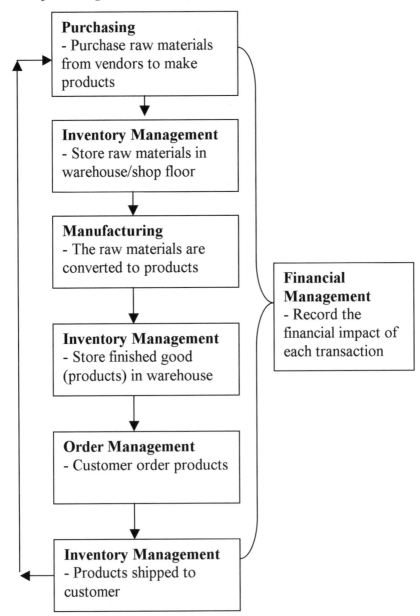

Stop Working!

Distribution Partner

Some distributors will also perform manufacturing functions for the products they distribute. If your distribution partner doesn't provide manufacturing, they should at least do all the distribution functions. It's possible to find individual partners for each function, but then you'll need to spend some time ensuring they integrate easily. For instance, if the order management partner isn't the same as your Inventory partner, you need to ensure easy and effective communication between both partners. In other words, when you receive a customer's order, the Order Management partner must be able to submit that order to the inventory partner, who will then fill the order within a reasonable, agreed-upon time.

Here's an example of what it would be like using different Warehousing (WH) and Order Management (OM) Partners

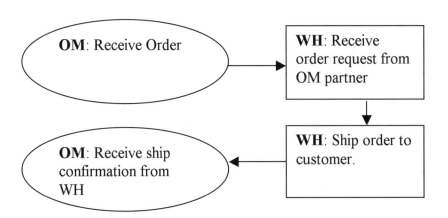

There are a variety of ways to facilitate communication between these partners. They include email, fax, EDI (Electronic Data Interchange), phone, and XML. Whichever method you select, you'll have to verify it works by testing the communication links. *Don't leave it to chance.*

The distribution process can be complex and expensive, and it may be time consuming to find the right vendors for your product. A distribution partner can be a great asset to your new business. They should provide all the services required to take orders, warehouse and ship your products, collect funds, and provide basic customer services.

These day to day tasks are time consuming if you do them yourself and costly if you have to build an infrastructure to perform these functions. To build the infrastructure you'd need employees, equipment, technology, and contacts. Not to mention established relationships with vendors to facilitate ordering discounted raw materials for your products. You'd need the technology to manage each function, plus the right buildings and physical infrastructure to house your employees, products, technology, raw materials and finished goods.

You should find a distribution partner in your specific line of business to facilitate these processes for you.

The value of a Distribution Partner

A good distribution partner offers a variety of benefits you couldn't provide yourself, such as:
- multiple ways to take an order
- unlimited warehousing capacity
- access to other distributors (and customers)
- lower cost shipping
- access to other partners.

Multiple ways to take orders

The primary ways to take orders today are via telephone, fax, email, EDI (electronic data interchange), XML, and online.

The most expensive way to take an order is by telephone, because someone has to be paid, even if you get no orders. If the employee receives only minimum wage you'd still need a minimum number of orders to justify the cost. According to the

Stop Working!

US Department of Labor, the federal minimum wage in the United States is $5.15 per hour. Hiring someone to take phone orders eight hours per day for a 40-hour week is $206. For one month, this is $824. Even if you have only one order for your product, your cost is still $824. When you add the cost of phone equipment, a monthly phone bill, office space, office equipment, and a variety of other overhead costs, your cost will be at least $1,000 every month. It doesn't take a lot of skill to answer a telephone, but that function alone at a minimum wage can cost you over $1,000 per month.

When you use a distribution partner you should make sure taking phone orders is part of their service. This service is called a *call center*. In most cases your cost for this service will be based on the number of calls you receive. Therefore, you may be charged $1 per inquiry phone call and $2 per order taken. If you have ten calls during the month you only pay $20 for the same service you'd otherwise pay over $1,000 for. Additionally, most call centers are open 24 hours per day to answer calls from customers and take orders. This 24 hour service is especially valuable if you sell products internationally where the time difference may be eight to twelve hours. When you're going to bed your customers may just be waking up.

Cost of hiring employee to take phone orders vs. using distribution partner call center

	Your Employee	Call Center
Calls Answered	10	10
Work hrs per month	160	160
$ Per Hour	$5.15	
$ Per Call		$2
Monthly Service Charge		$25
Employee Cost	$824	$20
Monthly Phone Bill, Equipment	$55	
Total Monthly Cost to answer 10 calls	**$879**	**$45**

Taking orders via Fax and Email

Your distribution partner should also have the ability to take orders via fax and email. Many corporate customers will only order your products through these routes, because they're traceable. Both these methods allow corporate customers to assign a Purchase Order (PO) for the purchases they authorize. A typical Purchase Order is printed, signed and faxed to the vendor. Your distribution partner must have a fax machine that's always available to accept orders any time of day or night. Once the order is received, it must be promptly processed by your partner.

Purchase orders can also be emailed from a corporate customer, another distributor or an end customer. Your business partner must be able to follow up with customers as necessary to get information required to complete the order and ship the products.

EDI and XML

Electronic Data Interchange (EDI) and Extensible Markup Language (XML) are different ways companies can automate ordering your products. This type of communications is often done when there's an established relationship between you and your customer, along with large, frequent orders. Large companies that process hundreds or thousands of transactions per day are more likely to use these methods. Both methods use a shared data format to transmit data between two computers.

Online

You must also be able to take customer orders online, so your distribution partner should also offer this feature. The feature may include your partner building an order taking web presence for you or allowing you to link your existing website to their order taking website. Either way, all orders should flow directly to them for processing. Once an order is received, it should be processed exactly like an order taken from any of the other listed methods.

Payment Methods

Your distribution partner also adds value because of their ability to take any form of payment. It's possible for you to create an online merchant account that will help you process credit cards, but it's easier to let your partners handle this aspect of the business. Your distribution partner should have a set transaction fee for each order they process for you, and that cost should include credit card processing as well as any other fees.

Unlimited Warehousing Capacity

A warehouse is a storage place where your products are kept until they're purchased by your customers. As the business expands you may need multiple warehouses from which to distribute your products. You may need a warehouse on the east coast of the USA to distribute products in that time zone and another on the west coast. As you sell internationally, you may need to have your products warehoused somewhere in Europe or central Asia so your customers can receive their orders in a reasonable amount of time and at a reasonable cost.

To build or buy your own warehouse would be very expensive, because you'd have to equip it with the right machinery, tools, people and technology. Your costs would include various unskilled warehouse personnel as well as skilled employees to handle production and inventory management (PIM). You'd need various technologies, such as a bar code scanning system and inventory and distribution tracking software. In most cases you'd require racks, pallets, containers, conveyors, lifts, and hand trucks.

Using your Distribution Partner gives you access to all this without the cost. You can select a partner with the best state of the art equipment and the most knowledgeable personnel at the most reasonable cost. You should choose a partner with experience in your particular area of business. This will ensure the right knowledge, the right equipment, the right warehousing conditions, and the best cost.

The cost of using your Distribution Partner's warehouse would include item such as:
- Warehousing space used
- Insurance for your products
- Shipping/processing cost per item
- Monthly service charge

You should calculate the total of these costs and divide by the amount of products you have stored in the warehouse to determine your cost per item. Various scenarios should be used when calculating this. Here's an example:

Example
Warehouse 5000 items. How much does it cost per item per month?

	5000 Items	Per Items
Space used	$150.00	$0.030
Insurance for your products	$20.00	$0.004
Shipping/processing cost per item		$1.500
Monthly service charge	$25.00	$0.005
Total	**$195.00**	**$1.539**

Based on this scenario, if you sold nothing this month your cost would be $195 for warehousing. Compared to the cost of having your own warehouse this is very inexpensive.

Wholesaler Discount
Retailers buy products at a discounted price referred to as the wholesale price. Your end customers may buy your product for $39.99 from your retailer, but in order for the retailer to make a profit they must buy the product at a discounted price from you directly or through your distributor. This discount can range from 20% to 60% depending on the situation. In many cases you'll be able to negotiate this discount amount, but sometimes the retailer demands a standard discount that's part of their profitability.

When you do pricing calculations you'll have to take this into consideration. Let's assume a discounted price of 30% for your retailer that's passed on through your distributor. The following is the revised calculation, including manufacturing cost, distribution costs, and wholesale discount.

Operational Revenue/Expense Worksheet

	5000 Items	Per Item	% Of Sales
Revenue			
Gross Sales	$199,950.00	$39.99	
Cost of Goods Sold			
Manufacturing			
Manufacture Product	$3,750.00	$0.75	1.88%
Distribution Charges			
Shipping/Warehousing processing charge	$7,700.00	$1.54	3.85%
Order processing charge	$10,000.00	$2.00	5.00%
Wholesale Discount			
30% discount	$59,985.00	$12.00	30.00%
Total	*$81,435.00*	*$16.29*	*40.73%*

Access to other Distributors and Customers

Distributors reduce your need for direct interaction to your end customers. This is possible because the distributors already have this access via their relationships with retailers. Distributors work with various other types of distributors, retailers, and sometimes end customers, and they operate within a network of networks. One distributor may have access to five major distributors and multiple small distributors. Those distributors may have access to other distributors, who will have access to a variety of retailers. The retailers will have access to the end customers.

These multiple levels of distributors and retailers give you instant national or global access to a customer base. The retailer already has a reputation and relationship with customers. Through this relationship, customers will trust the products the retailer offers.

Stop Working!

A customer may buy a product in Wal-Mart or walmart.com for instance, but will not buy the same product on your website, even if it's less expensive. That's because the customer trusts Wal-Mart and doesn't know anything about you. To get your product in a store like Wal-Mart however, you'll probably have to go through a distributor Wal-Mart trusts. This distributor will be a part of the distribution network that feeds directly to Wal-Mart as well as other stores.

Imagine the difference between selling your product in Wal-Mart stores and selling from a website few people know about. Even if customers find your site, they don't have the confidence you'll protect their credit card information or their products will arrive on time and as expected. Compared to that, imagine a customer who walks into Wal-Mart, sees your product, picks it up, and pays for it at the cash register. The customer doesn't know or care who makes the product or where it was made. All he knows is that it fits a current need and he's buying it from a retailer he can trust.

To gain access to an infinite number of customers, your distributor must work with retailers that sell product to your consumer base. If they don't directly have access to the retailers you want, then they must work with other distributors who have that access. Part of your agreement must include your ability to access massive retail chains via your distributor.

A coffee bean distributor should have access to Starbucks or any other major coffee retailer; clothing distributors you work with must have access to the major clothing stores; book distributors must have access to major booksellers; records and CD distribution partners must have access to major record stores.

Once you've connected to the right distribution partner, you'll sell products to retail establishments through the distributor. In many cases, the retailer will automatically carry your product in their catalogs because they use the distributor's catalog. In other cases you may have to request that they purchase your product from the distributor. Either way, you're already in the door. *In most cases, if you're not with a distributor the retailer works with they will not consider carrying your product.* You will therefore have to pick your distribution partner wisely.

In essence, you benefit from a pre-existing relationship between distributors and retailers. This is a classic wholesaler (you), distributor (your partner), and retailer relationship. All you have to do is plug into this network to get exposure to the massive customer base of these retailers.

Stop Working!

Your Distribution Network

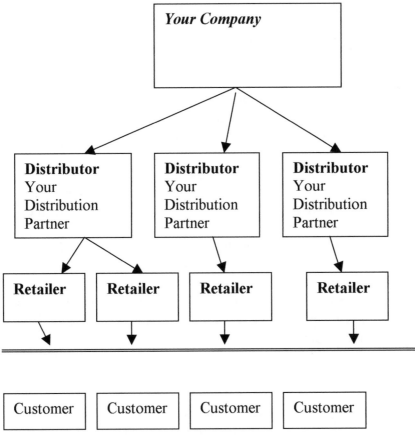

Demand Driven Network

We refer to this network as a demand driven network. Entire schools of manufacturing talk about demand driven manufacturing as well. The main concept is to build the network and let your customers' demand drive all your other business processes. This concept works as follows:

Retailers advertise on a regular basis to drive customers to their stores. You will also market your products to end customers as well as retailers. The customers will buy your products because of their value, and also because they trust the retailer from whom they're purchasing your product.

When your product is purchased, the retailer's inventory level drops and they need to order more products to replenish (replace) the sold goods. They place an order with the distributor who carries your product.

The distributor ships the product from a warehouse to the retailer's warehouse or store. After shipping products, the distributor now has a lower inventory and will order more products from you. Based on the system you've established with them, you can approve the order and pass it on to your manufacturing partner.

The manufacturing partner creates new products and ships them to the distributor. Your role in this entire process is to simply approve the manufacturing of more products – or you can set up pre-approved replenishment agreements by signing an agreement between your manufacturing partner and your distribution partner to pre-approve new manufacturing orders with specific replenishment quantities.

As part of this process you can establish a maximum and minimum inventory level with your distribution partner for your product in their warehouse. If your inventory falls below a certain amount, the distribution partner must reorder a specific quantity of new products from your manufacturing partner.

The value of doing this is that as demand for your product increase, your sales increase, your inventory decreases and your distributors are able to replenish their inventory levels without your direct intervention. This also drives the manufacturing process based on demand for your products and without your intervention – hence the term *demand driven manufacturing*.

Your inventory levels will never be greater than your *Maximum Inventory Level*, you control when new products should be ordered by your *Reorder Level*, and you control how many new products should be ordered by your *Reorder Quantity*.

You will never have too much inventory, nor will you ever run out of inventory. These numbers can be changed at will if demand for your product decreases or increases over time. And of course, you can be on vacation in Jamaica while all this is happening.

The following shows an example of setting up an inventory replenishment system with three different distributors, ensuring that your distributors never run out of inventory and that they will never have too much inventory. Having too much inventory is costly, because you have to pay for the manufacturing and storage of the products. Having too little inventory is also bad because you never want to loose and order because of lack of inventory.

	Distributor A	Distributor B	Distributor C
Maximum Inventory Level	5,000	4,000	700
Reorder level	2,000	2,000	500
Reorder quantity	3,000	1,000	200

Maximum Inventory Level – The maximum amount of your product that will be stored in the warehouse

Reorder Level – Once your inventory quantity falls below this amount, you should order more products to avoid running out of inventory.

Reorder Quantity – The amount of products to be reordered to replenish your inventory. The reorder quantity plus the reorder level must be less than or equal to the maximum inventory level

Lower Cost Shipping

Your Distribution Partner will most likely ship in bulk to other distributors or to retailers. By doing so, they get discounts from various shipping firms like UPS, and FedEx. In many cases, they will have free shipping to other distributors or retailers that they send frequent shipment to. This discount is passed down to you. To ship 200 of your products will cost significantly less if they do it than if you were to do it yourself. This discount shipping cost can be passed on to your customers, or used to offset your other expenses. Either way, it will often be significantly less expensive to have your distributor ship your products than doing it yourself.

Purchasing (Procurement)
Raw Materials

You should not have to worry about purchasing raw materials to manufacture your product. Your manufacturing partner should have the relationships necessary to purchase these at a discount, because they make other products similar to yours. They will already have relationships with various vendors and suppliers of the raw materials required to manufacture your products.

If you're in the book printing business, your manufacturing partner will have relationships with vendors who provide paper and ink. Since they buy this in bulk from these suppliers, their cost will be significantly lower than your cost to purchase the same raw materials.

You should be able to work with your manufacturing partner to determine the materials that will be necessary to manufacture your product. They will have a Bill of Materials (BOM) listing all the raw materials required to manufacture your product. In many cases you won't need to get that detailed. When you give them your prototype and specify your manufacturing order, they should be able to deliver a complete product at a discounted price.

As always, be careful to ensure the standard of quality you want for your product. The manufacturing partner should be able to create a sample product before mass production begins, so you'll know what your product will look like and the quality of the product before full production begins.

Supplies

You will also need daily supplies for your business. I recommend buying from wholesalers or memberships discount warehouses whenever possible. Some of the popular membership discount warehouses are Costco, BJs, and Sam's Club. You can normally find anything from computers, pens, books, food and nearly anything else you need for your business. The main idea is that you'll pay less than retail cost by buying in bulk quantity.

Managing your Distribution Network

Once you've created this network of partners, you need to manage it. Large companies spend millions of dollars trying to do this. I've mentioned some of the various technology used in an earlier chapter. Fortunately, you won't have to spend even a dollar to do this.

Remember your partners have already made this capital investment. They already have the technology required to manage the warehouse, customer orders and customer tracking, and handle sales. All you have to do is request access to this technology and they will give it to you. In fact, before getting into any contracts or agreements you should verify this as a fact with your partner.

Distributors will have this technology and will gladly give their partners access to it because it reduces the amount of questions they have to answer from you everyday or every week.

By empowering you to check your sales figures yourself, they don't have to do it. By allowing you to track shipments online, they don't need to hire someone to give you that information. This technology is already in place as part of their infrastructure, and they're more than willing to share it with you.

You'll need access to a variety of online reports answering the following questions:

1. What is my available inventory?
2. How many products did I sell today?
3. What are my gross sales for the day?
4. What are my net sales for the day?
5. What are my sales figures for this month?
6. What are my year-to-date sales figures?
7. Who is buying my product?
8. Which region of the country or world are my products being shipped to?
9. What kind of customer feedback am I getting?

Some distributors will give you access to very detailed information, while others will give you more of a summary report. Either way, all you have to do is ask for it. The format will most likely be via a webpage. Your distribution partner will give you a URL link to their extranet with user and password information so you can log in. They'll probably restrict your access so you can only view information pertaining to your company. Additionally, you should build a customer database from this. A standard format most computer applications can use is csv (comma separated values). This format separates each value (name, address, zipcode etc) with commas. You can load the data into Ms Excel, MS Access or a contact management application. Once you have your customer list you can use it to inform customers of other products you may offer, or provide support to your customer base.

Stop Working!

Internet, Intranet, Extranet

I personally believe the Internet is one of the most brilliant tools invented in the last century. We're all familiar with this technology in one way or another. Sadly, we're mostly familiar with the failure of the dot com revolution that died as fast as it rose. As I mentioned earlier, the dot comers had the right idea, but the wrong execution. The following are current ways the dot com technology is currently applied.

Internet

The Internet uses an unsecured world wide web (www) frontal approach to information. By knowing a specific URL or address, one can access information posted on the Internet. Additionally, this address can be found by using search engines such as Google, and Yahoo.

eCommerce, the ability to sell your products online, has failed for most businesses, and there are a variety of reasons for this. One is trust, another is lack of financial resources, and a third is bad business skills. This book addresses some of these reasons and shows how an Internet business combined with the right strategic partnership can be successful.

Research is one of the most beneficial uses of the Internet, which contains tons of information on virtually any subject you can imagine. Additionally, the Internet is an excellent way to expose information about your products and services. Once your information has been discovered, then a dialogue may start with you and your prospective customer.

Intranet

Intranets use the exact same technology as the Internet. The primary difference is that Intranets are computer networks used within organizations. Virtually every major organization will have their own Intranet through which they share information internally. This information is not exposed to the

Internet community. Companies may therefore have Intranets with portals to a variety of corporate information. A portal is an index page that links to other pages. www.yahoo.com is a classic portal application that links to other applications. Corporations have these types of portals as well. The information they link to may include corporate phone lists, corporate applications (like ERP and CRM), announcements, corporate stock prices, internal job opportunities, health plans, security policies, and a variety of other information that's restricted to corporate employees.

Extranet

Extranets use the same technology as the Internet, with the only difference being the level of access. Extranets typically give some limited secured access to corporate information to customers, suppliers and strategic partners who receive a user id and password to gain access. The access that your business partners will give you to their internal information is via extranets. After logging in with your user and password information, you enter a corporate secured server. The URL of the web page will probably start with http://secure or http://server instead of http://www.

An extranet gives you access to part of a corporation's secure server, allowing you to manage your business online. By partnering with this organization you now have access to millions of dollars worth of technology without having to worry about the cost.

Show Me the Money

Distribution

========

Eye Contact Media, Inc. (www.eyecontactmedia.com)

Your distribution partner will be one of your most important business relationships, and should not be taken lightly. Spend as much time as possible researching potential partners. Read all the fine print of every contract before you sign, and especially watch for exclusivity clauses. Many distributors only work with exclusive contracts. If you sign an exclusive contract you should be sure it's worth it.

We have a variety of distribution partners, giving us access to retailers and end customers all over the world. We found these partners by doing extensive research on the Internet. We had specific requirements based on the types of networks we needed to access. As a small company, many distributors won't want to work with you. The ones who *will* work with you may not have the networks you need in order to grow a successful business.

As we did our research we recognized more requirements that we hadn't thought of in the beginning. Each distributor wanted an exclusive contract. We didn't mind signing such a contract, but we needed to know it made sense to lock ourselves into that kind of arrangement. In the end, we didn't sign an exclusive contract. Instead we continued our research until we found distributors we could partner with who already had existing relationships with retailers and other international distributors with whom we wanted to do business.

Once we found these potential distribution partners we requested quotes for their services. Although most of the information we needed was available on their websites, prices were not. We also found that by searching on the name of the distributor we were interested in we could uncover related information as well as competitor information..

I have to say, this process can be laborious, and I thank my wife for doing a majority of this research. We sent a request for a quote to each of the distributors who met our criteria. Some answered and some did not.

We quickly wrote off the organizations that didn't respond to our request. If they were unresponsive to potential new customer, how would they be responsive to our customers when we become their partners? We did follow up emails and phone calls to the ones we were interested in.

Price was always important and we looked closely at the numbers. A price per item was always calculated. A service that cost an extra $1 had to be taken seriously. The logic is that if we sold one million books, that extra $1 would cost us a million dollars.

Service and responsiveness were also important. I don't like to be in business with anyone who doesn't find it important to respond immediately to me or my customers' requests and issues.

After we selected a few candidates, we had telephone meetings where we discussed a variety of issues, concerns and opportunities. We had a list of questions we felt were important to understand.

The partners we selected offered us a range of services and access. Since the goal of Eye Contact Media has always been global sales and distribution of our products, we focused heavily on how these distributors would help us achieve this goal.

Our distributors were also partners with a variety of other global distributors, forming on of the largest distribution network in the world. Therefore, we're able to compete with Mega-organizations in our field. Our products sit on the shelves beside the products of these giant organizations.

Stop Working!

Our network integrates the financial, supply chain and manufacturing processes. The integration is seamless and we can access our accounts through our partners' extranets, allowing us to manage our business from anywhere in the world with little effort.

From this, our clients have a variety of ways to order our products – including bookstores as well as online. Customers are able to call an 800 number 24 hours per day, 7 days per week to order our products. A live customer representative is always available. Customers can link from our corporate website to the distributor's E-commerce website, where our partner captures the order, processes it, and professionally ships the product – regardless of where the customer resides. Customers can also order our products via fax or email.

Our products are warehoused in our primary distributor's warehouse facilities after they're manufactured, then they're moved to the warehouses of other distributors in the USA and different regions of the world. As the products are ordered, they're shipped to warehouses of the retailers, then into the hands of customers. This gives us virtually unlimited warehousing capacity. Because of this it takes only a few days for customers to get our products anywhere in the world. We're using warehouses in the USA, Europe, and Asia yet we own no warehouses.

This entire process is demand driven. Our responsibility is to increase demand for our product. Each purchase of our product by customers initiates this demand flow. The flow is automatic and requires no intervention from us. Even though we have an entire industry working for us, we hire no employees. We create jobs by virtue of our relationship with our partners, but we don't have the responsibility and liability of employees.

By virtue of our role as a wholesaler, our products are sold to retailers at a discount. This allows retailers to make a profit, and we also make a profit. The discount is passed through our distributor to the retailer, and the retailer determines which part of this discount they want to pass on to the end customer.

We have competent people working 24 hours per day, seven days per week in order taking, warehousing, manufacturing, and retail outlets – but without the burden of a payroll. They run the daily business processes of our business, while we manage the direction of the business.

We also have access to technology. I can look at a variety of warehouses online and know exactly what the day's sales and demand is. I know what the exact inventory level is daily for each key warehouse.   I keep track of this to make sure products are automatically ordered when a warehouse quantity gets low. I make sure the reorder quantity is sufficient to meet the expected demand for the coming weeks.

If the automated process of reordering isn't sufficient I email my distribution partner and ask them to order more products to meet this demand. They follow through because they are excellent partners.

I love using this technology because I can do it from anywhere. I travel a lot and don't carry a laptop anymore. Actually, I don't own a laptop anymore. If I'm away for a week visiting my parents I can use their computer to check the status of my business. I can do the same from my favorite Internet café in Amsterdam, or one of those nice Internet cafes in Thailand or New York, depending on where I am.

Because of this technology I can manage my business without being tied to a specific location or office.

There's a cost for all of this, of course. All the numbers were presented up front before I signed any deals with distributors, because I don't like surprises. I used MS Excel to crunch the numbers and see what the true service cost of my distributor would be for each book we sold. I used a revenue/expense worksheet like the one presented throughout this book. I will always be profitable because I know that all my costs are a small percentage of my gross revenue.

vConcepts, Inc (www.vconceptsinc.com)

Globileware is licensed to our partners, who use a distribution network to market and sell the software in a variety of countries. They're responsible for sales and distribution of the product. Think of this as the original type of relationship Microsoft had with IBM. Microsoft provided the technology and IBM sold computers with the Microsoft technology included.

There are a variety of different types of licensing agreements between the Globileware organizations and other vendors. Since the technology is a middleware product, users may use the product without knowing that they are using Globileware. The product will typically be licensed to consulting partners or technology partners. These partners brand the technology as their own, offer the technology as a mobile solution to their clients, and implement the technology. From this, our partners are able to offer a sophisticated technology to their client base, receive sales and consulting revenue for the product, without doing any product development. From this relationship, our partners are happy, their clients are happy, the clients' customers are happy – and of course I am happy.

You can learn more about Globileware from the www.globileware.com website.

Rohan Hall

Chapter 9

Create Demand

———

This book is about how to create and automate a demand driven Agile enterprise. Once the infrastructure is created you will need to have ways to create demand for your product. Fortunately, because of your distribution network – your retailer will already be creating demand for your product.

The retail part of your network will constantly be doing promotions, advertising, and marketing of their retail outlet. A part of their job is to drive customer into their stores or to their online stores. Your retail outlet may be stores you find in malls, on main streets, or popular online stores. They will have name recognition and easy access. By simply having your products in these retail outlets, you will have sales of your products.

Once this relationship is established, however, you'll want to take your sales to another level. A part of this will be brand and product recognition. Therefore when a potential customer walks into the retail outlet they should pick your product over the competitor's product displayed next to yours.

Brand recognition is the reason people choose one product over another in a similar situation. Nike, for instance, usually sells more shoes than the competition because of their powerful brand. You don't need to spend as much money as Nike does, but you should do some level of marketing and advertising.

Marketing, Advertising, Sales
Marketing, advertising, and sales are often used interchangeably, but the three functions are fundamentally different. Here are some of these differences.

Marketing
The goal of a marketing campaign is to give consumers information about your product or brand. This is also referred to as promotion. Many marketing avenues are free, such as a book review in a national newspaper. You don't pay the newspaper to write the review – they simply must believe your book or product is of interest to their readers.

Common areas of marketing include radio interviews, newspaper product review, magazine product reviews, news articles about your product, and news stories about your industry.

Even though it costs nothing to utilize these services, gaining access to the people who would do these reviews, interviews or articles for you can be difficult. That's why you need a Marketing Partner.

A marketing partner will have access to media sources that will promote your product. For example, if you want magazine reviews about your product, your partner should provide contacts with various magazines that will do this for you. If you'd like to promote your product via radio interviews, they should be able to contact a variety of radio stations and schedule interviews.

This network is what you pay for when you hire a marketing firm to help promote your product or company.

Therefore, you should only hire such a firm if you're confident they have the access you need and will get the results you want.

At times you'll hear marketing firms say "Hey, I can't promise anything." I wouldn't do business with these firms. Marketing firms are usually expensive and can eat up 40% or more of your business costs. I don't expect to pay a lot of money and get the same results as if I'd done the work myself. Therefore, I recommend you do extensive research on firms that do promotions in your business area. I wouldn't use a book promotion firm to promote my new software product, because the media outlets used by the book promotion firm are different than the media outlets a software company would use.

There are many other ways to market and promote your products. One such way sends spam email and pop-ups to the computers of unsuspecting consumers. I've never known anyone who appreciated that type of invasion or harassment. Even if you're able to sell some products with that method, you'll lose the good will to a huge range of potential customers – and besides that, it's illegal. I discourage this type of marketing.

That said, I do believe that having an opt-in list of customers that have expressed an interest in receiving product information from you is an effective way of marketing your products. As you surf the web you will notice that most businesses now require you to *sign up* for their website if you would like free information, products and opportunities offered by their business. I regularly receive email newsletters from a variety of business and technology magazines, national newspapers including the *New York Times* and other businesses that offer products and values that I find important. What is important about this is that I requested this service by signing up on their website for these newsletters.

I find the information provided by these organizations as a value, not spamming or harassment. If at some time I decide that I do not want to receive emails from these organizations I simply unsubscribe to their services.

Your website should provide this service. The internet is an amazing opportunity to create a community of people who are interested in your products or services. People who are interested should be given the opportunity to learn more about your offering via informative newsletters or new product release. By doing this, you are building a relationship with your customer base, you identify people who are genuinely interested in your product, and you also create a forum to directly communicate with these interested customers.

Your opt-in list of interested customers will become more valuable to you over time. Imagine having a list of thousands of people who have requested that you send more information to them about your product or services? It is an opportunity to give more to this group of customers via free information or free products.

You can also find people to promote your product for you, such as well-known athletes or community figures. The basic idea behind this type of promotion is a word of mouth recommendation from someone people trust. You can get a similar effect by using established newsletters and magazines in your product market. This may require that you write some articles relating to your product and submit them for publication. The audience reading this will receive a direct recommendation from you – an expert in the field.

Friends, customers, colleagues are the most effective way of promoting your business however. Don't be afraid to ask people to recommend your product to others. In fact, if you find this book valuable please recommend it to all your friends.

Has this every happened to you? You go to work or school, someone told you about a great movie they saw or a great book they read. What did you do? You went and watched the movie or bought the book. So don't be afraid to ask the people who enjoyed your product or benefited from your product to recommend it to others who may benefit from it as well.

Stop Working!

Advertising

Advertising is usually a service, whereby you pay someone to say or print specific information about your product. You may have an advertising campaign printed in newspaper all over the country. The ad will give basic information about your product as well as were consumers may be able to buy it.

For small advertising campaigns you don't really need an advertising firm. However, I recommend you research your options on the Internet as well. There are often discount advertising brokers who sell advertising packages to various newspaper and magazine outlets. For a discount price, these firms give you the opportunity to run an ad in a group of regional newspapers, or magazines that target a certain market.

Operational Revenue/Expenses Worksheet

	5000 Items	Per Item	% of Sales
Revenue			
Gross Sales	$199,950.00	$39.99	
Cost of Goods Sold			
Manufacturing			
Manufacture Product	$3,750.00	$0.75	1.88%
Distribution Charges			
Shipping/Warehousing processing charge	$7,700.00	$1.54	3.85%
Order processing charge	$10,000.00	$2.00	5.00%
Wholesale Discount			
30% discount	$59,985.00	$12.00	30.00%
Create Demand			
Advertising & Marketing	$10,000.00	$2.00	5.00%
Total	$91,435.00	$18.29	45.73%
Net Revenue	*$108,515.00*	*$21.70*	*54.27%*

Sales

With your distribution network you don't need sales people, because your retailers will already have salespeople to deal with customers. Your main job will be setting up the network and helping create demand for your product. Once you create the demand and the customer seeks out your product via retailers, the entire demand chain will begin. The retailer's sales people help customers purchase your products, and the sales flow through to the distributor to your bank account.

Test your demand network

Now that you've created your network you must test it in order to be sure customer orders will be processed in a timely manner. You need to know your products will be shipped as promised and experience what your customers will go through when they buy your product, whether from a retail outlet or online.

The best way to do this is to make a purchase and pay close attention to the details of the transaction. If you're doing the purchase online, here are some things you should look for:

1. Were you comfortable giving your credit card number online? If not, then why?
2. Was it easy to find your product online?
3. Was there enough information about your product to give a good understanding of its use and value?
4. How many clicks did you have to make from the point of purchase decision to completion of the transaction?
5. Was the purchase done on a secure server (***https***:// uses a secure server - ***http***:// is not secure)?
6. Is the online store capable of taking all major credit cards?
7. Did the online store clearly state the cost of the product as well as shipping and handling charges?
8. Were you given a delivery date for the product?

9. Did you receive a follow up notification/confirmation email from the online store?
10. How did you feel at the end of the transaction?

For Brick and Mortar stores
1. Were the sales people friendly?
2. Were the sales people aware of your product?
3. Were the sales people knowledgeable about the benefits of your product?
4. Was it easy to find your product?
5. Was your product in stock?
6. What physical condition was your product in?

Once you've purchased your product you should use your distributor or retailer's extranet to observe your product flow through the demand chain. If the product is shipped to you, you should be able to tell when it was actually shipped from the warehouse. When you receive the product you should inspect it to verify it's in good condition and all required shipping documents are included with the package.

Test your demand network in as many ways as possible. Once you know it works as expected, then all you have to do is find new ways to create demand, manage the network, and build more products to add to your network.

Show Me the Money

Create Demand

========

Eye Contact Media, Inc. (www.eyecontactmedia.com)
Our #1 priority in year one was to build our network. Toward the end of that period we also focused on creating demand for our product by using a marketing partner. This effort resulted in countless radio interview and magazine promotions.

One area we found to be interesting is the level of word of mouth promotions we received from our customers. Since our product is sold on a variety of online bookstores, our customers have the opportunity to give feedback and commentary online, and we believe this word of mouth activity has driven demand from these satisfied customers. Positive discussions about our product have appeared on a variety of bulletin boards, newsletters and chat forums as well.

Information about our product seems to be everywhere on the Internet. The book can be bought in bookstores and on countless websites on the Internet in a variety of countries.

We believe this has contributed significantly as well to the demand for our product to its current bestseller status in a variety of markets domestically and internationally.

Demand creation is a continuous process. We plan to have a variety of planned demand driving activities every year for each product we sell.

We will also continue using a variety of marketing partner to help drive demand for future products.

Stop Working!

vConcepts, Inc. (www.vconceptsinc.com)

While Eye Contact Media offers mass market consumer products, vConcepts offers Tier 1 enterprise integration products and solutions. The marketing is therefore significantly different. vConcepts and Globileware customers are large organizations and governments. Our approach is more of a direct relationship approach via our relationship with vendors that service these specific industries. These vendors, through their established relationships, will recommend our products and services.

Our marketing effort therefore focuses more on specific targeted organizations instead of a general broad consumer market. A combination of our specific marketing efforts and marketing done by our strategic partners make our products and services well valued by our customers internationally.

Please check our websites for more information at www.vconceptsinc.com and www.globileware.com.

Rohan Hall

Chapter 10

Create New Products

_____

After you've created your product, tested your network and created a market demand, you've effectively created your Agile organization. Now you must continue creating demand for your product through your marketing or advertising partners. You can also create this demand yourself if you know how to do it.

At this point you've created a stream or residual income that will continue flowing without any further intervention from you.

You may want to create or acquire additional products to introduce into your network. Theoretically, the more products you have in your network, the more money you'll make. You're the best judge of how many products you need and how often you will need to introduce a new product.

I personally like the Microsoft strategy. They own a handful of products, and every few years they release new versions of the same product – effectively making the old products obsolete. The new products are simply an improvement over the old ones.

You see the same with ERP and other technology products. Every few years they release newer versions of the same products. Customers want to have the latest and greatest version of the product and will spend the money to buy or upgrade. Customers who don't buy the newest version will eventually lose support for their old versions.

How can you apply this concept to your market?

A book you introduce to a market can have a 2nd edition or a follow-up book, using the series concept. The Harry Potter books use this formula well. I read every Hardy Boys book while growing up and was fascinated by Agatha Christie's Hercule Poirot detective series. When creating a series you'll be able to use the same distribution channel, strategic partners, and manufacturer you used for your original product. Everything is already in place – you simply need to introduce the new product.

One of the most successful films of late was *Lord of the Rings*. They created a product and two others after it. Their customers liked the first film and couldn't wait for the second and the third. *The Matrix, Harry Potter, Spiderman* and *Kill Bill* used a similar formula.

You aren't limited to intellectual property however. In 1988 I bought the first Hyundai automobile that hit the United States market. At the time it was just a new, cheap foreign car and all I could afford. Today they have an entire series that's anything but cheap. They created a network and distribution channel in the United States, introduced an initial product, and then added more products on a regular basis.

You need to determine what it means to be rich. How much money is enough money to stop working? Your decision will determine how many products you want to introduce through your network.

Some products will be phenomenally successful, while others may flop, but you can minimize your losses and maximize profits by using an Agile organization..

Stop Working!

The more successful products you have in your network, the more successful you'll be.

Revenue for 4 products in your network

	Monthly Revenue	Yearly Revenue
Product A	$8,000	$96,000
Product B	$14,000	$168,000
Product C	$3,000	$36,000
Product D	$6,000	$72,000
Total	*$31,000*	*$372,000*

Remember as well that once you have these products in your network you have virtually nothing to do except create demand for them – much of which will be done by the retailers, while the core business processes are carried out by your partners.

You'll have to continue managing your business, however, and this is a job you'll never want to give up because it takes only a few minutes per day.

Therefore, assuming it takes two years for you to create (or buy) and market four products. The scenario above shows four products yielding $372,000. This is $372,000 you've earned without having to work with the exception of managing your business a few minutes per week. You have this money and all the freedom to enjoy it in the world. For one person this might be extreme wealth. For another, it's barely enough to live on. Regardless of what it means to you, you've created cash flow to spend as you please. From this point on you simply need to maintain or increase demand and introduce new products at will.

Show Me the Money

Create New Products
========

Eye Contact Media, Inc. (www.eyecontactmedia.com)
      At the end of our first year we felt we'd sufficiently built and tested our Agile structure. Our products flowed easily through a variety of distributors to our retailers and then on to their customers without our intervention.

      We had good banking and financial business processes and were comfortable with the access to technology our partners provided to help manage our business.

      Our sales had improved every month since the product initial release and the business was quite profitable.

      This year we'll be adding more items to our portfolio, including products of our own creation as well as those we have the right to market and publish. We'll continue adding products each year.

      The great thing about this is that our work doesn't increase for each product added to our business, nor do we need to hire more staff. We add the product to our established network and sit back while our partners do all the work.

      Our partners are happy to do the work because they make money. We're happy they do it because it's less expensive than hiring staff and it frees our time so we can focus on our core competencies – producing new products and focusing on strategic direction. We're helping grow the economy without burdening ourselves in the process. The level of work we personally have to do therefore doesn't increase with the number of products we release. The pre-release work in building the product is substantial, but afterwards the day to day business activities don't increase for us. This is possible because we're looking at the same reports provided by our partners daily. The only change is that instead of one product we now see sales, inventory levels, demand and financial information for multiple products.

Another product we will be releasing this year is an excellent recipe book from my wife Sylvie. I'm a very lucky guy in many ways because Sylvie is simply a gem. She's an amazing woman who was born and raised in the Auvergne region in the center of France. She's multi-lingual and has backpacked a good part of the world, as I have. We both love traveling and eating great food from all corners of the world. During her travels Sylvie has collected recipes from France, Spain, Ireland, Thailand, The Middle East, the Caribbean just to name a few places.   She has a fascinating talent of creating meals that mixes French elegance with exotic herbs and spices from different countries all over the world.

I've convinced Sylvie to create a book of these recipes and to tell the stories of some of her travels and her life growing up in France. Look for her book called *Simple and Simply Delicious Recipes*, by Sylvie Rocher.   I'm sure you'll enjoy every meal.

Work diminishes dramatically after product release

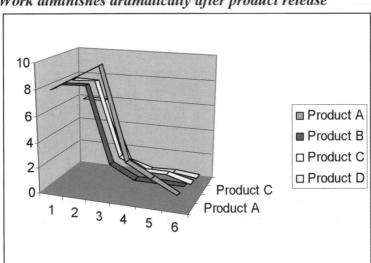

Illustration – Our personal time commitment is high during product creation for each product. We can easily spend eight to ten hours per day for each product we create. This phase can last for weeks or months, depending on the product.

Once the product is released our time commitment diminishes to less than an hour per day. This doesn't change with multiple products. We look at the same reports for one product or ten. It doesn't take more than a few minutes each day to review and respond to occasional issues that occur. An issue might be a higher than expected demand for a product that would call for our intervention via email to increase product inventory for a particular warehouse to meet demand. But product reordering is automated, so this will rarely occur.

Stop Working!

Rohan Hall

Section III

Technology & Resources

Rohan Hall

Chapter 11

Technology

_____

I talk a lot about technology in this book because technology is one of the core strategic elements you'll find in every business today. It's impossible to avoid. Those who try to ignore this fact won't survive long in today or tomorrow's economy. The days of hanging a sign on your door to make the town aware of your services have long passed. Everyone from manufacturers, distributors, accountants, and lawyers use some form of technology to their benefit. You must do the same.

Even though I'm a big believer in the value of technology I don't believe you have to spend a lot of money to harness the benefits of technology. As a small business you need some basic software applications to run your business. Your partners will have the real expensive stuff. Use their expensive technology and save yourself tons of money.

A key question you should always ask yourself when you buy technology is "What are the current standards being used for this type of technology?" This isn't an area where you want to be creative or too leading edge. The market turns as quick as the wind blows. Therefore, you want to invest in technology you know will work and is compatible with most other technology out there. I suggest this because you want your investment to last several years.

Hardware
Desktop Computer

For a small business your choices are limited. You'll have some kind of windows based personal computer or an Apple brand computer. Unless you're a programmer or have experience with other types of systems like Unix, Linux etc, I suggest you avoid these systems. Though excellent in many ways, they have a larger learning curve and you'll have difficulty finding standard applications for them.

People who buy Apple computers seem to be passionate about it because Apple offers a variety of standard desktop publishing features and applications. Apple also offers many of the applications you'll find on PCs. However, if you walk into most businesses or if you're in an Internet café while traveling you'll see more PCs than Apples.

My personal preference is PCs because they're inexpensive; I use the same technology at home, at work, while visiting clients, visiting friends and family, and traveling. I enjoy the consistency.

I recommended in an earlier chapter that you buy the least expensive new module you can find. The brand is pretty much insignificant. The same technology is used to make each brand and sometimes the same manufacturer makes the components. The manufacturing practice used are pretty much standard for this technology. You may want to look at features such as a DVD Writer, CD, disk capacity, memory etc. However, for most small businesses the standard off-the-shelf PC will do just fine.

Stop Working!

Laptop Computer

A laptop computer (often also called a notebook computer) is really a desktop computer you can carry around. The components and casing are smaller and the price is larger because of the convenience. Unless you travel a lot you should probably just get a desktop. Laptop screens can sometimes be small and hard to read and the keyboards can be funny and difficult to use. You should take the time to test the feel of these machines before you buy them.

Laptops differ by weight as well. An extra pound or two could make a difference when you're traveling with the machine. Laptop features such as external disk drive and the kind of equipment it works with can also be challenging. You should do as much research on the machine as possible before buying one. A laptop with comparable equipment and performance as a desktop can cost twice the price of the desktop. It becomes a choice, but that choice is primarily based on how much traveling you do and the level of access you'll need to your data.

As a business professional I traveled with laptops for years, literally all over the world. This gave me access to corporate data, email and personal data I kept on the machine. Much of that data is now available online. You can read your personal email from a variety of free online email services. You can also access your email and other important data from your corporate extranet for most organizations. Your important data files can also now be backed up and accessed online from anywhere. Companies now allow secure extranet access via wireless connection from your cell phone or PDA – similar to the services we provide with out Globileware application. If you don't have this access then you can always find an Internet café or an outlet like Kinkos that gives you 24-hour technology access for a cost. Either way, you should weigh the need for a laptop versus a desktop before making this capital expenditure.

Printer/Fax/Scanner

A variety of manufacturers are now making a combo all-in-one device that includes a printer, fax and scanner. These combo devices are great because they save you the cost of buying each device individually. Additionally, you don't have to worry about how to connect all these devices or what device is compatible with others. Installation is extremely simple.

A *printer* is necessary for any business. As more things become digital, there's a need to print more documents. The all-in-one devices offering a laser printer will be significantly more expensive than ones with an inkjet printer. As a small business you really don't need a laser printer unless part of your product offering requires this. Most people won't be able to tell the difference between a good inkjet document and a laser-printed document. Plus a majority of your printing will be for internal use only, since most document-sending today is done by email.

Fax technology is pretty standard today, so you don't need anything expensive to do this. The all in one combo solution provides a basic fax machine you can use from your home/office. Even though you can use the fax for both sending and receiving, I primarily use my fax for sending documents.

Internet fax services have also become very popular over the last few years. When you sign up for this service, you are given a fax number that is tied to your email account. You can give this fax number to anyone to fax info to you. The cool feature about this is that the fax someone sends to your fax number goes directly to your email. Therefore, if I give you my fax number and I travel to China I'll receive my fax as long as I have access to email – which I will since I also use an online email service.

The clear value of this is that I don't need a physical fax machine to receive fax. My fax appears in my email inbox like any other email I receive. There are a variety of available internet fax services. Some charge you a fee to have a fax number with a local area code. Others offer the service free for a limited amount of time, and then you'll have to upgrade. Search around and pick the deal that's best for you.

Scanners are becoming increasingly valuable as we digitize more information. If you don't have a digital camera, a scanner is the next best thing. You can scan any document you need to keep long term (such as legal documents) and save the document on your hard drive. You can then back up these documents on a CD, DVD or external hard drive for permanent record keeping. You can also scan pictures from your regular camera or old printed pictures, then share them with others or make them part of your website as you create an Internet presence.

Software
You'll need to either own or have access to certain types of software. I'll make the distinction in this section for you.

Software you need to have
In our world of high-speed communication you need a variety of software applications as tools to manage your business:
- Word processing
- Email
- Spreadsheet
- Backup & recovery
- Anti virus & popup blocker
- Financial

Word Processing
You use a word processor to create documents such as resumes, analysis documents, communication letters etc. A variety of word processors are available, but MS Word is the standard.

Spreadsheet
I use my spreadsheet program to do anything I'd normally do with my calculator. In fact I have a nice calculator and rarely use it anymore. Spreadsheets are good for anything having to do with numbers. I prefer spreadsheets to calculators, because I can actually see what I'm doing and save the results to use later. For instance, I use my spreadsheet to keep track of certain budget items and financial projections. The financial worksheet used throughout this book was done on a spreadsheet. You can use other software to do this, but I like the freeform simplicity of a spreadsheet application. MS Excel is the standard for spreadsheet today.

Email
Email has undergone amazing innovations in the last few years, and it connects the world like no other application. Practically everyone I know today uses some form of email. What's great about email is that it's free and simple to use.

Free Email is primarily for personal use, even though many businesses use it as well. Search the web for "free email" and you'll find thousands of results. Two leading free email services are yahoo.com and MSN/hotmail.com.

There are also ***quasi-free*** email packages offered by web hosting companies when you purchase a web-hosting plan. A web-hosting plan would include the ability to build and host a website. Many of these vendors package in a low cost or free of charge Post Office Protocol (POP) email service. The way this works is that they store email on their email server then give you access to the email via a webpage or via a client application such as MS Outlook. You get a user and password to access the email via a web page or you can configure you client application (MS Outlook) to read their mail server to receive or send email. You can also use a free email service like Yahoo to read these types of POP email servers.

Client based email applications however is the standard for the corporate world. Corporations have their own secured email server. All emails that go into or leave the corporation are stored on the corporate email server. The email is scanned for viruses and is often permanently stored for legal reasons. If you have sent or received an email from the company you work for you should be very careful of the content. Even deleted email can be backed up for the corporate use. The general policy of many companies is that email is the property of the corporation. Therefore if you are ever in trouble and evidence is required, emails you have sent or received at work can be potentially used against you. The primary client based email application used today is MS Outlook.

Wireless email is also gaining in popularity. You can now read email from your wireless cell phone or PDA. This is still considered an emerging technology and you will see this feature offered by all wireless devices over time. It is mainly used by corporations currently but is gaining a large consumer base as well.

Antivirus & Pop Up Blocker

I will always remember 2004 as the year of the viruses. New viruses have been released almost on a weekly basis, and each new release seems more destructive. Most of the viruses are merely annoying, but others will delete files and attempt to crash your computer. Computer users with only a basic knowledge of computers will suffer the most. Your annoyance of not knowing what to do and the fear of losing your work can be overwhelming. Good antivirus software is a requirement of everyone who owns a computer that's connected to the Internet.

In addition to destructive viruses, we all face annoying, offensive materials in the form of pop up applications. By clicking a link these *applets* (small web applications) take over various functions of a computer. In my definition this is just another type of virus. However, various virus software makers don't provide a solution to these annoyances. Here are some questions for you to ask about antivirus software you're thinking about buying:

1. Does it auto-scan to stop the virus *before* it infects the computer?
2. Does it auto-update virus definitions for new virus threats?
3. Does it scan emails for viruses?
4. Does it stop pop ups, spyware, and adware type viruses?
5. Does it auto clean/kill the virus?
6. Does is stop all the known types of viruses?
7. Does it scan IM (instant message) downloads for viruses?
8. Does the company have online information for you to learn more about current virus threats?

Backup/Recovery

Backup/recovery software is a companion to your antivirus software. Use this to automate backup of your important data files nightly or at least weekly. I've had two computer crashes in the last two years for completely different reasons. Some of the reasons you could unexpectedly lose data include:

- You're attacked by a virus that wasn't stopped by your anti-virus software
- Your computer is hacked (invaded) by someone
- You installed a software that was incompatible with your operating system and corrupted and crashed the system
- You installed hardware that corrupted your system and crashed it
- Your computer was faulty and it crashed

There are many other reasons why you may unexpectedly lose data. You'll need to purchase backup/recovery software you can use to store all your data files. With these programs your data can be stored on CDs, DVDs, external hard drives or another computer. If your system crashes, you can re-install your program files and recover data files from your backups.

There are also various vendors that now offer automated online backup for your system. In these cases, the data is stored on the vendor's secured server instead of on your CD, DVD or external hard drive. This 'offsite' backup is good especially for disaster recover or if you need access to your data from a remote location. You may consider combining these various methods to have a more comprehensive backup/recover solution.

Financial

This was mentioned in an earlier chapter, but you'll need financial software to manage your business. You should use a cash basis for accounting, download your transactions from your bank to the financial application and use standard reports to manage your business. These reports can be sent to your accountant who will use them to complete taxes for you. Most of this software is simple to use and takes only a few minutes to set up.

Website

You should have an Internet presence in the form of a web site, but you don't need to spend a lot of money on this. The days of spending thousands of dollars on building a website are gone. You can build one yourself with a variety of web authoring software. You will need to pay for a web hosting account. Research this because these accounts can be very expensive or inexpensive. Many provide free email and tools to build websites and ecommerce sites. With the website building tools available today, building a site can be as easy as typing a document in a word processor.

Also, if you want to have a really cool website but are clueless about designing such an application there are now a variety of website template applications now being sold on the web. You can buy these templates, modify them and use them as your website. You save countless hours from trying to do this your self. Templates come designed based on a variety of business types. Therefore, you can easily find templates for computer stores, book stores and a variety of other product and service related businesses.

Software you need to use, but shouldn't buy

Unless you keep the following business functions you shouldn't need to spend any money on software to support them. However, you should have access to reports from these software applications via your various partners.

Order Taking

This is the software your partner will use to take orders from their customers. Your relationship with them will determine your level of access. Some partners will be able to create a data file of your monthly customer transactions, while others will give you only online access or a paper report. Either way it's important you make the effort to get and keep a list of customers who purchased your product so you can use this customer base to market future products.

The reports will include customer names, addressed, phone numbers, email addresses, products purchased, quantity purchased, dollar value of purchase etc. This is easier to attain when your products are sold on the Internet because the product is then shipped to the customer. Where the product is sold in stores it will be more difficult to capture this information.

Inventory Tracking

Inventory tracking software is used to follow your product from the warehouse to customers. You'll need access to inventory levels and shipping information. This software is important because it shows your current inventory levels, and they should tie into your sales figures.

Sales Tracking

In a consumer environment, this is the same as the order taking software. Once an order is confirmed or shipped, it's considered a sale. In cases where you have access to retail sales information, you'll see a combination of orders taken and inventory on the same summary report.

Rohan Hall

Chapter 12

Professional Services

Business & Technology Consultants
There will be times when you need help with things you simply don't have experience with. This may be to create certain business strategies, develop technology, create your product prototype, etc. You'll have a choice of hiring someone or using a consultant with expertise in a specific area.

In general, I believe a small business can't afford most or all of the employees they hire. The decision to hire or not should be purely financial. You're running a business and you will need to think about what is best for the business.

Get an Expert
The cheapest resources can often become the most expensive. Get an expert with years of experience to perform the task you want done. The person should have a tract record of

success with this, along with references. If possible they should also be able to show examples of their work.

The best professional service providers are not necessarily the most expensive, and the least expensive individual isn't always the best value. You'll have to put together the total cost of ownership via a needs assessment for the project. Here's one way to look at it:

You want to build a technology project. You have two offers:

	Hourly Rate	Time Estimate (hours)	Total Estimate
Consultant #1	$50	85	$4,250
Consultant #2	$25	143	$3,575

Which is the best deal?

The answer is, you don't know. It will depend on the consultant's verifiable experience. You should check experience and background to make sure they have the skills you need. I would want to know why one consultant needs 143 hours to do what someone else estimates at 85 hours. Also, if I want this done within two weeks (80 to 100 hrs) then I would have to automatically eliminate Consultant #2. The main idea here is that the total cost should meet your needs.

You would therefore have to determine what your needs are before you can make a good decision.

1. How much are you willing to pay for this project?
2. When do you need to have it done?
3. What benefits will you receive from the completion of this project?
4. If the project isn't completed on time, can you charge penalties against the consultant – how much and what are the conditions?

5. If the project is late, what is your backup plan?

As you go through this *needs assessment* you'll be more prepared to select the best candidate to perform this service. Stay away from the idea that the cheapest deal is the best deal, or the most expensive consultant must be the one with the most experience. Do a needs assessment, extensive research, and pick the provider who will best provide the services you want to meet the timeframe and resources you can allocate to the project.

Use the following steps when selecting a consultant to provide a service:

- Develop a needs assessment document of what you want to achieve, including your goals, deadline, and budget.
- Research to find a list of consultants who provide this service. You can find service providers on the Internet, through advertisements, in the phone book, and through word of mouth.
- Interview individual consultants or consulting groups to see their capabilities.
- Create a short list of those you are interested in
- Request a quote or proposal from them for the service you're seeking.
- Compare their proposal with your needs assessment to make sure they'll be a good fit.
- Do reference checks.
- Secure their services through a contract. Build in a penalty or exit clause to protect yourself if things don't go as planned.

Project Plan

Depending on the service you are requesting you may want to have a project plan from the consultant. This is typical for technology projects. You may secure a consulting group to build a new technology that may take a few weeks or months to complete. You should request a plan that shows deliverables, deadlines, costs and resources. This plan should be available in a detailed form as well as a summarized format.

The project plan will be your guide to insure that the project is moving on as scheduled. If target dates are being missed regularly you will need to make sure that the project is not at risk by speaking to those who are responsible. This is your management tool that will ensure a project scheduled for eight weeks at a specific cost doesn't go for twice the time and twice the cost.

Accountants and Attorneys

Accountants can be a valuable part of your business, because as your business grows so does your tax liability. The nature of your business can also introduce a variety of tax complications.

As a business owner, you may have several business expenses that can reduce tax liability. The main idea is that costs incurred in developing or running of your business reduce your net revenue, which is what you're taxed on as a business owner. A good tax accountant is essential to help you understand tax laws and how you can reduce your tax liability

A good tax accountant can save you money by applying deductions entitled to you by the federal government.

Attorneys can also be valuable to your business, and also very expensive. The hourly fees charged by most attorneys can be exorbitant, depending on the firm they work for. The junior person in a prominent law form can charge over $250 per hour, while the senior person might charge over $400 per hour.

We need attorneys for a variety of reasons, but there are ways you can receive the service you want without the cost.

Using Attorneys for Document Creation

Imagine having an attorney create a contract document for you. To help you out, he assigns the project to the junior attorney. The junior attorney takes one and a half days to create the document. Upon reviewing the document you decide there are things you'd like to change. You have a meeting with the attorneys and outline the changes you want them to make. It takes 3 hours to make the change, and you're finally happy. How much money do you think you've spent? Let's see:

Senior Attorney $450/hr, Junior Attorney $250/hr

Attorney cost to create contract document	
Initial Meeting (2 hrs - Sr. Attorney)	$900
Develop contract (12 hrs - Jr Attorney)	$3,000
Review meeting (1 hr Sr Attorney, 1 hr Junior Attorney)	$700
Change contract (3 hrs Jr Attorney)	$750
	$5,350

You would have spent $5,350 to develop a contract you *may* use only once, and you could have found it free or inexpensive on the Internet. This isn't a good way to spend your hard-earned money.

Note however, that I started out by saying attorneys can be valuable for your business. The problem here wasn't the attorney – he did exactly what you asked. The problem is how you used their services.

The first thing to realize is that most of the legal documents you'd pay an attorney to develop are already available somewhere on the Internet. Various websites allow you to download documents for a cost, and other sites provide documents at no charge. You'll need to search for these documents, verify that they aren't copyrighted, and then modify them as needed. Remember that someone already paid an attorney to create the document, it's probably technically legal.

Only after you've changed the document to meet your needs should you secure the services of an attorney. At this point you don't need someone to develop the document; you simply need someone to review it to make sure it's accurate, legal, and representative of what you want it to do. The difference is cost could be as follows:

Senior Attorney $450/hr, Junior Attorney $250/hr

Attorney cost to create contract document	
Initial Meeting (free - Sr. Attorney)	$0
Review/Modify contract (3 hrs - Jr Attorney)	$750
	$750

The initial meeting is free because you don't have to give a detailed explanation of what you want to have in the document. You're inquiring about the fee and explaining your needs. They can write the changes they suggest and you can make the changes yourself, or they can modify the document if you have it in electronic form. You can also email them the document, but first make sure you get an estimate regarding the amount of time it will take for them to do this review.

By doing this you would've saved over $4,000 on this one document alone. Imagine the cost savings with multiple documents over the coming years!

Using Attorneys for Advice

You must always remember that attorneys get paid by the hour. It's best to always be as informed about the subject at hand before seeing an attorney. You're paying for his expertise, but if it takes four hours to understand their advice instead of one hour, you still have to pay for the entire time they give you. Also, doing extensive research on the subject matter enables you to ask more intelligent questions, comprehend the answers, and use the attorney's time more wisely.

Show Me the Money

Professional Services
=======

Eye Contact Media, Inc. (www.eyecontactmedia.com)
No consultants have been used for Eye Contact Media.
We used a template to create our website. The entire website was
created in a few hours.

Attorneys
We haven't used any attorneys for our legal requirements.
After years of being in business I can read as well as write my
own contracts or I get one for about $10 or $20 from the websites
that offer this service. You don't need to be an attorney to write
a legal contract. More than that however, I prefer to use the
attorneys of the entity I'm doing business with, because they
always have a contract ready for every purpose. My job is to
read the contract and strike anything from it that I don't agree
with. If an important issue isn't covered, I make sure they
include it in the contract. The entire legal fee is their cost, not
mine.
I can do this with the greatest confidence, because after
years of being in business I realized that most contracts are
boilerplate. This means the terms and conditions are often
identical. If I were to get ten contracts from ten different
partners, the paragraphs might be shifted around and the words
slightly different, but a close review will show the same terms
and conditions.
When I read these contracts I use a yellow highlighter to
mark things that don't sound right or I don't agree with and then
ask that they be removed from the contract. I know I have that

right and have no issue with executing it. I also know what I need in the contract, and if it isn't there I send an email with the exact text I need. This is a part of your original contract negotiation. You never want to sign a contract you don't agree with or can't live with. To change a contract after you've signed it can be a laborious and expensive task. Therefore you must identify the changes you require *before* you sign.

These changes require a rework of the contract, but the rework is their cost, not mine. I don't pay that $250/hour – they do. This is why I spend almost no money on attorneys.

When they send me the reworked contract I read every word again with my yellow highlighter, because this contract is in fact a new document. I may not be very trusting, but I never sign a contract unless I've read every single word. If it's reworked five times, I read every word each time. This is good practice and saves lots of money in the long run.

Because of people like me, companies have learned over the years to do boiler plate contracts. The contracts are typically standard for that industry and will usually not have anything that's extremely unfair, because if they do they know that it will cost them money to rework.

I also don't use attorneys for copyright, trademarks, patents or any such services. You can patent or trademark your work at the US Patent and Trademark office online (http://www.uspto.gov/) for a small fee. You can copyright your work also for a small fee online (http://www.copyright.gov/) at the US Copyright office.

Your risk in doing this is that you may miss a legal loophole that an attorney can help you with. I agree with that. To mitigate this risk you can simply do a search at these sights for similar patents, copyright, trademarks close to the ones you're trying to create. If you've invented a new mouse trap find other patents on mousetraps filed by large companies that can afford really expensive attorneys. Review the document they filed and apply it to your invention.

Stop Working!

If you don't know anything at all about patents, trademarks, and copyrights, the government websites provide a lot of details regarding this. Read the details and increase your business intelligence. Once you've become more knowledgeable you still have the option to decide if you can in fact do this yourself or if you'd like the help of an attorney.

I don't want to sound like I'm anti-attorney, because I believe they provide a valuable service. However, I do believe the level of service small businesses receive from attorneys is typically not the same as large businesses. It makes practical business sense. Attorneys will make more money from a large organization than a small start up business. To get the same level of service the large companies get you'll need to spend the money they do.

A large organization may spend tens of thousands of dollars to file a patent. You can't afford this because you don't have the budget. Does that mean that your work should not be protected? Or worse, does it mean you should accept a lesser quality of work but still spend thousands of dollars?

Unfortunately, you'll often find that attorneys simply file the exact forms you can get online for free or for a small cost – they're provided by the government. You should call your attorney and ask what it will cost to patent a product, copyright your work, submit a trademark application or start a business. Don't be surprised if their fees make you feel like the poor stepchild. I love this country and I love the way our government uses the Internet. I'll always respect the dotcomers for initiating this technology (which is also an invention of the government – research ARPA sometime if you're curious). Why? Well, here are the current fees required by the government if you use the referenced websites to protect your intellectual properties

Intellectual Property Protection

Agency	Cost
US Patent and Trademark Office (http://www.uspto.gov/)	
Filing fee for Utility Patent (Small Entity)	$385
Effective April 1, 2004	
http://www.uspto.gov/web/offices/ac/qs/ope/fee2004apr01.htm	
File a Trademark	$335
http://www.uspto.gov/teas/eTEASpageA.htm	
US Copyright Office (http://www.copyright.gov/)	
Register a copyright	$30
http://www.copyright.gov/docs/fees.html	

The fees are a fraction of what an attorney would charge you to file these documents. With some research and understanding of the requirements for these documents, you can do it yourself and save thousands of dollars in the process.

If you're not comfortable doing this yourself, then you should seek the help of an attorney. Even if you decide not to do it yourself, it will be a wise investment of your time to at least become knowledgeable about the information provided freely on these website so you're armed with factual information when you speak to your attorney.

Accountants

We do rely on our accountant for tax related matters. He is always available and responsive. I normally send emails regarding questions or issues and receive a response the same day or the next day. If there's a perceived emergency I call him directly.

I rely on accountants because the more money one makes over the years, the greater the tax burden you have to carry. It will freak you out the first time your tax liability for one year is more than one or two years combined from your previous annual salary. Can you imagine paying more taxes in one year than your total income for one or two prior years?

To minimize your tax burden while helping your business grow, the Internal Revenue Services (IRS) has provided a variety of legal tax deductions. But tax laws change yearly, and the way these deductions can be applied is different based on a variety of factors.

I have a good understanding of the tax laws that apply to me, but I have no desire to learn the details or keep abreast of the yearly changes. That said, I also don't want to miss taking advantage of any tax situation that applies to me. And last but not least, I want to make sure I minimize the possibility of any tax mistakes or issues. For those reasons I use the best accountants I can find. My accountant charges a reasonable fee for excellent work. I use my financial software to gather the required transactions and he uses this information to prepare my tax filings.

Tax Software

In all honesty I've never used business tax software to do my taxes. I did use a personal tax software several years ago to do my personal taxes and I didn't feel I benefited in anyway from this.

As you start to develop businesses your taxes become more complicated. You have to deal with revenues from Business A versus Business B, revenue from the United States versus foreign countries, personal investments versus business investments, employee taxes and unemployment compensation, and state taxes versus federal taxes. Each of the documents required seems to come with heavy fines and late charges if they aren't done right. I'm not confident that the tax software will save me money or time. That's why I don't use them.

I think a knowledgeable tax accountant could use this software to his or her advantage – and I'm sure they do, but it's a challenge I've chosen not to take on. If this is one of your strengths, then it's a wonderful thing.

However, the cost/savings ratio I get from my accountant is worth every penny.

Chapter 13

Stop Working

How much money do you need to stop working?

The answer will be different for everyone. The question is similar to how much money do you need to be rich?

In an earlier chapter we talked about 5-year goals. In that chapter I said that one of the primary goals to have is wealth. I also stated that you should define what wealth means to you, and that your definition of wealth will change as you acquire more money.

One common standard used to measure wealth in our society is net worth. Net worth is the total amount of assets minus your debt.

Net Worth Calculation

Assets	
House	$350,000
Car	$35,000
Jewelry	$5,000
Savings	$25,000
Total Assets	*$415,000*
Liability (Debt)	
House	$250,000
Car	$25,000
Credit Cards	$45,000
Taxes	$10,000
Loans	$25,000
Total Liability	*$355,000*
Net Worth	*$60,000*

The above calculation makes people feel comfortable when they look at their financial situation. If our goal is to stop working, however, this calculation tells us nothing of our true financial position. People with this financial position go to work stressed everyday with the fear of being laid off because they know they wouldn't be able to pay their bills without selling all their assets.

To determine your true financial position and understand if you're able to stop working you'll have to do a calculation commonly referred to as your cash flow position. It's a common financial calculation that every business uses. Many business owners look at their cash flow statement every day with the first cup of coffee, before doing anything else.

The calculation focuses more on revenue and expenses than on balance sheet data (assets and liability).

Cash Flow Calculation

	Monthly	Yearly
INFLOWS		
Revenue (ABC Corp)		
Product A	$8,000	$96,000
Product B	$14,000	$168,000
Product C	$3,000	$36,000
Product D	$6,000	$72,000
Revenue (XYZ Corp)	$65,000	$780,000
Total Revenue	*$96,000*	*$1,152,000*
OUTFLOWS		
Expense (ABC Corp)		
Product A	$3,600	$43,200
Product B	$6,300	$75,600
Product C	$1,350	$16,200
Product D	$2,700	$32,400
Expenses (XYZ Corp)	$16,250.00	$195,000
Other Expenses	$6,000	$72,000
Total Expenses	*$36,200*	*$434,400*
TOTAL CASH FLOW	**$59,800**	**$717,600**

Your monthly cash flow would therefore be $59,800. This will always need to be a positive number. If it's a negative number, then you aren't able to meet your monthly expenses.

The value of having an efficient Agile business is that you're able to better manage your expenses while increasing your revenue. The lower you can keep your expenses, the better your cash flow will be.

Your cash flow will be increased by your increase in demand. The more demand, the more your revenue will increase.

Debt kills your cash flow, which is why I've stressed throughout this book to keep away from debt. The monthly payments you have because of debt will not increase your revenue. Instead, debts increase the expense you have to pay every month, which has a negative impact on your cash flow.

The assets listed above in the net worth calculation are practically useless when determining if you can stop working. Owning more of those assets does you absolutely no good in determining if you can stop working unless you owe no debt on those assets or unless you 're able to make regular income from those assets. While you're paying for them, they are simply a drain on your resources.

Whether a house is paid for or not, it will cost you money. A car that's paid for still cost money to insure and maintain. All these costs must be added into your cash flow calculation.

That's why a net worth calculation is useless. The actual value of a net worth calculation comes into play if you want to borrow money from the bank. The bank will want to know that if you don't pay them back, they can take away these assets, liquidate them, and recover the funds they loaned to you.

To stop working, however, you'd have to sell those assets and live on the street.

It's like winning the Lottery

We've all heard the stories of people winning the lottery and end up broke and penniless in a few years. Even worse are the people who end up broke and owe a lot of debt. Most of these people will never have the opportunity to ever make that kind of money again and will be forever in debt unless they choose to file bankruptcy.

A question I often ask of people who are seeking to get rich is:

If you won the lottery today worth $5 million dollars and you're given two choices: Option #1 – take a lump sum of the winnings; Option #2 – take annuity payments for 30 years, which option would you take? Most people go for Option #1. The thought of having five million dollars in their bank account is just too tempting.

Stop Working!

I don't gamble but if I did, I would take Option #2. The reason is simple. Option #2 pays me for 30 years without me having to do anything to earn that money. Every month, every year for 30 years the checks would keep coming while I kick back on a beach somewhere in the world.

Here's the calculation based on winning the Ohio lottery for a $5 million jackpot. I don't live in Ohio, but they have a very nice online calculator[5] for their lottery system.

Winnings $5 million

CASH OPTION	
Present Day Cash Value	$2,200,000.00
Federal Taxes (27%)	$594,000.00
State Taxes (3.5%)	$77,000.00
One-time Net Cash Value Amount	*$1,529,000.00*

ANNUITY PAYMENTS (30 YEARS)	
Annual Payments	$166,666.66
Federal Tax (27%)	$44,999.99
State Tax (3.5%)	$5,833.33
Net Prize Amount for 30 Years	*$115,833.34*

After present value calculation and taxes you will have $1.5 million dollars left from your five million-dollar winnings. Most people have no idea how to invest this newfound wealth and will lose it within a few years. They'll lose the money because they've never had this much cash and don't know how to invest it wisely. Investment is also a matter of market fluctuation. Even mutual funds were losing between 40% to 75%

---

[5] Source: http://www6.state.oh.us/drafts/lot/numbers/cash_option.htm

of their value in 2001. It will take years to recover much of those losses.

People will also lose this money because they'll spend it. It's very tempting to have over $1 million in the bank and not buy the largest house possible, along with the most expensive cars for yourself and your family. The money will be spent on jewelry and vacations. It will be spent on luxury items and services you were not even aware of before winning this money. Once this money is gone, it's gone forever.

I believe the best investments are those that give me recurring revenue. I would take the 30-year payment option because I know that even if I spend every day for the next 30 years at the beach making sand castles I would still make a yearly income of $115,833 – after taxes. For the next 30 years I would have the peace of mind that I wouldn't go broke and I would work only if I chose to do so.

I could choose to spend the money or invest it. As long as I didn't create a negative cash flow situation (more monthly expenses than my annuity payments) I'd never be broke. The payments would just keep coming for the next 30 years.

After having a stable long-term income source, you'll want to maximize your cash flow situation. To do this you should get rid of debt – all your debt. There's no freedom like a debt free life.

If I'd won the lottery above and accepted the annuity payments, my first mission would be to pay off all my debts and, while living comfortably, reduce my expenses to the minimum. I would owe no credit card bills, no car payments, and as soon as I could – I would pay off my house. I don't need the largest house; I simply need a comfortable home. There are certain monthly utility bills that will never go away. However, at the end of the month my cash outflow would be at the minimum. My inflow would then be directed to savings or other investments that would increase my inflow.

Having your Agile business works the same way. You're creating a pipeline that will pay and keep on paying. Your first product may yield $40,000 per year. That may not sound like a lot, but if you have four products averaging that much per year in net cash flow you would have the equivalent payments as our lottery example above ($40,000 * 4 products = $116,000). You don't need to win the lottery to live like a lottery winner; you just need the right business strategy.

The two best business strategies, in my opinion, are my own business and rental real estate properties. I like having my own business because of the indefinite wealth potential –long term and immediate. I like rental real estate because of the long term stability and cash flow potential. These are the two investments that will put money in my pocket indefinitely with a minimum amount of daily effort.

It's like the Oprah Show

I went home for mothers' day just last weekend. I had just finished the transcript for this book and was excited to show it to my parents. They were delighted. They thought it would be able to help a lot of people develop their financial potential. During the discussion about the book my mom said, "It's like the Oprah Show". I said, "What do you mean?" My mom is a super fan of Oprah. She continued, "You can help so many people with it. Plus, isn't that the way Oprah made her money?"

Suddenly out of nowhere my mom was pulling out books and magazines about Oprah's life and her wealth. I was quite impressed. I already knew that Oprah was a billionaire and that she owned Harpo Inc, but I got educated by my mom on all the charity work that Oprah did. I was most impressed by the Oprah Angel Network and that she raised over $17 million for children and various other people over the world.

I had to think about it as I flew back home. I decided to check some of the information my mom had told me on Oprah's website (www.oprah.com).

Was Harpo Inc. an Agile business?   Let's see:

- Oprah becomes the host of the Oprah Winfrey Show in 1984
- She formed Harpo Productions, Inc. in 1986.
- Harpo Productions takes over production for the Oprah Winfrey Show (the Product) in 1988
- The show is distributed by King World (the distributor)
- Through its distributors, the Oprah Winfrey Show went global. According to Oprah's website her product is shown in 110 countries.
- Oprah then created new products for her company. These include movies; a cable show called Oprah After the Show; and O, The Oprah Magazine[6]
- Each day, week, and month that these products are created she is creating new products for her market.
- Since she is owner of the company, she gets direct cash flow from the sale of these products. Since these products are the intellectual property of their owner, she will get paid indefinitely.
- Oprah's work is the creation of her products and the strategic focus of her organization. Her partners then distribute them globally.
- 15 years after starting Harpo, Oprah is a billionaire.
- Oprah does not need to work another day in her life. Oprah works as a matter of choice.

Again mom was right! Harpo Productions Inc, is Agile. I called her the next morning and told her so. I also told her that I would mention our little conversation in the book. She was delighted. So am I.

Be an Angel
I've always believed in helping others. My parents taught me the pleasure of being able to positively affect the lives of

---

[6] Source: www.oprah.com

others. It is part of the reason why I wrote this book. It is a part of my constant goals. To be able to give is a gift within itself. I have to admit as well that I am also quite inspired by Oprah's Angel Network[7].

I believe the children are the future. The quality of life they can live and the impact they can have on the world can be affected by their financial position. I mentioned earlier in the book that when I was 19 years old I had two jobs while I went to college and started my first business. One of those jobs was as a computer teacher at an elementary school. My students ranged from Kindergarten through sixth grade as well as the after school program that included adults, some of which were grandparents that were curious about this new emerging technology. I enjoyed teaching my students how to write computer programs. Even fourth graders were writing computer code on the new computers of the day – Radio Shack TRS-80 and Apple IIe. Children enjoy learning and enjoy the challenge of learning new and exciting information.

Today I think it is important for children to learn about business and finance before they get caught up in the rat race. I would like for them to know that they have a choice.   My goal is simple – teach people how to be more financially intelligent with a special focus on the younger generation. Towards this goal I will provide free copies of this book to a variety of schools and universities. It's clearly not possible to give the book freely to everyone. If you are not on the list of schools to receive this freely, I have authorized our distributors to provide a special discount of this book to any educational institution that request it. Log on to our website at www.eyecontactmedia.com to get more information about this program.

I believe that anyone can be an angel. I do believe this book can change one's life. This may be your opportunity to be an angel by helping someone to change their financial outlook.

---

[7] The author and publisher of this book have no affiliation with the Oprah Winfrey Show, Harpo Productions or Oprah's Angel Network. The author does find Oprah to be pretty cool, however.

Get a copy for a friend or tell them about this book if you believe it can have a positive impact on their life.

Stop Working

The decision to stop working will be a personal one. Creating a greater cash flow and stabilizing it over time will make this decision easier.

If you have a product with increasing demand that yields a good and constant cash flow, you really don't need to work. You only need one such product. For Bill Gates, that product was DOS, which evolved into the product now known as Windows. He didn't stop working however, and for that reason he's now the wealthiest man in the world. However, many businesses need multiple products to gain the cash flow required to stop working. Even with massive cash flow, many individuals will never stop working because they love business and the challenge and excitement of conquering new markets.

I find myself somewhere in the middle. I'm fortunate to have two different businesses in two separate markets that generate a significant amount of cash flow. I enjoy both businesses and will always work. A high net worth or a high long-term cash flow doesn't really change this for me. I just love the challenge of doing what I do.

What does change for me however is *how* I work or *how much* I work. I created the Agile structure from a variety of existing business concepts. The Agile structure for business isn't an invention – it's an organizing principle. It's important because it gives me the opportunity to do what I like and to do it the way I like to do it. Therefore I can write as many books as I want, build as many software applications as I like, and create as many companies as I like without being tied to the corporate rat race. I can work one hour, zero hour, or ten hours if I choose. I do things on my own terms.

I also have the privilege of making a good living. I get to have as much time as I like to spend with the people in my life I care about. Effectively I've stopped working, because I don't have to go somewhere to make a living anymore. Life is good and it remains interesting.

I'm going to Egypt, then France, this summer with my wife. We'll be gone about a month. I'll find an Internet cafe in both countries where I can check my email, sales, and inventory. I'll do it every few days in between the pyramids, the desert, and then the Alps. My bank account will have more money in it when I return than when I left, and I'll have some checks waiting in the mail as well. I'm really not worried about my business when I'm gone because I have the best strategic partners working hard every day and the best customers buying my products every day. They're doing all this for me so I can continue enjoying my life.

Wealth for me therefore is about freedom! It's about the personal freedom gained from financial freedom. I'm happy to say that today I do enjoy this freedom. I hope to continue being this fortunate throughout the rest of my life. I wish this and all *your* other goals might become a reality for you as well.

Rohan Hall

Appendix

Global Economies

_____

The global economy is your path to wealth as a business owner. You will need to use this to your advantage as a CEO. I've included for your use some of the largest global economies today. Use this information wisely to expand your business.

To find more details about these countries as well as any other country in the world, check the website of the United States Central Intelligence Agency – The CIA (www.cia.gov). Think about it: Who knows better than these guys about what's happening in the world today?

The CIA's World Fact Book contains economic, social, political and other information about every country in the world. I check this website for the _secret intelligence_ on any country I want to do business with, or countries that I plan to visit. You should do the same.[8]

Economics 101

I hated my economics class in college. I really made every effort to stay awake, but the class was just too boring. I barely passed the exams. The professor just didn't understand that economics was about making money and getting rich. If he could have expressed how we could all get rich from understanding economics, then I'm sure everyone would have looked forward to his class.

I'm not an economist, but I think I understand a bit about making money. One thing I know is that if you don't understand world economics you're limited regarding how wealthy you can become. I'll try at this point to explain a few basic economic terms you should have learned in college. These terms will help you understand what the whole fuss is about macro and microeconomics. You get to understand the big picture (macroeconomics) and apply it to your daily lives (microeconomics).

You'll also get an understanding of why jobs are continuing to leave the shores of the USA, Japan, and Europe to countries like India and China – and why they will continue to leave.

Consider this your Economics 101 course. It's important because you have to be able to see the big picture before you can appreciate what's happening in your daily economic life.

Economic Dictionary

Gross Domestic Product (GDP) – This is the total amount of money a country makes. The CIA uses a Purchase Power Parity (PPP) calculation as its method to estimate the GDP. The GDP of a country is similar to the Gross Revenue of a company.

---

[8] Note: I have no affiliation with the CIA. I just think they have a very cool website with fascinating information. The source of the data used in this segment of the book is the CIA World Factbook at www.cia.gov

Stop Working!

Understanding the GDP of a country is important because you want to do business with countries with the largest GDP. The more money the country makes, the more they have to spend. Doing business with companies with high GDP is similar to doing business with companies with high Gross Revenues. These are the companies that will typically show up on the Fortune 500 or Global 500 list.

GDP – Per Capita – This is the GDP divided by the country's population. This number is important because this provides an average of the purchasing power of each individual in a country. This of course assumes an equal distribution of production (or wealth), which is never the case, but it does give us a basis of comparison when we think of countries. Here's an example:

	GDP	Population	GDP Per Capita
American Samoa	500 Million	70,260	$8,000
Gibraltar	500 Million	27,776	$17,500

Notice that even though both countries have the same GDP, the GDP Per Capita is significantly different. The residents of Gibraltar have twice as much money to spend for their products and livelihood as the residents of American Samoa. In which country would you want to sell your products, based on these numbers?

Population – The estimated number of people living in a country. The greater the population of a country, the greater the GDP should be. Think of your own household. If your gross income for a year is $50,000 and two people live in the house, you can live fairly comfortably. Your per capita income would be $25,000. However if your population increases by an additional eight family members and your income remains the same, then life can get a little tough. Your per capita income would now be

$5000. This is the same problem faced by many countries: it's called poverty!

Poverty = High Population + Low GDP

Gross World Product (GWP) – This is the sum of all the GDPs of the world. You add the GDP of every country in the world to get this number.[9]

---

[9] The CIA's World Fact Book
(http://www.cia.gov/cia/publications/factbook/index.html)

The World

	Gross World Product		Population		Per Capita
World	49.00	trillion	6.3	billion	$7,900

Population:
6,302,309,691 (July 2003 est.)

Religions:
Christians 32.79% (of which Roman Cath olics 17.33%, Protestants 5.62%, Orthodox 3.51%, Anglicans 1.31%), Muslims 19.6%, Hindus 13.31%, Buddhists 5.88%, Sikhs 0.38%, Jews 0.24%, other religions 12.83%, non-religious 12.53%, atheists 2.44% (2001 est.)

Languages:
Chinese, Mandarin 14.37%, Hindi 6.02%, English 5.61%, Spanish 5.59%, Bengali 3.4%, Portuguese 2.63%, Russian 2.75%, Japanese 2.06%, German, Standard 1.64%, Korean 1.28%, French 1.27% (2000 est.)
note: percents are for "first language" speakers only

Economic Overview:
Growth in global output (gross world product, GWP) fell from 4.8% in 2000 to 2.2% in 2001 and 2.7% in 2002. The causes: sluggishness in the US economy (21% of GWP) and in the 15 EU economies (19% of GWP); continued stagnation in the Japanese economy (7.2% of GWP); and spillover effects in the less developed regions of the world. China, the second-largest economy in the world (12% of GWP), proved an exception, continuing its rapid annual growth, officially announced as 8% but estimated by many observers as perhaps two percentage points lower. Russia (2.6% of GWP), with 4% growth, continued to make uneven progress, its GDP per capita still only one-third that of the leading industrial nations. The other 14 successor

227

nations of the USSR and the other old Warsaw Pact nations again experienced widely divergent growth rates; the three Baltic nations continued as strong performers, in the 5% range of growth. The developing nations also varied in their growth results, with many countries facing population increases that erode gains in output. Externally, the nation-state, as a bedrock economic-political institution, is steadily losing control over international flows of people, goods, funds, and technology. Internally, the central government often finds its control over resources slipping as separatist regional movements - typically based on ethnicity - gain momentum, e.g., in many of the successor states of the former Soviet Union, in the former Yugoslavia, in India, in Indonesia, and in Canada. Externally, the central government is losing decision-making powers to international bodies. In Western Europe, governments face the difficult political problem of channeling resources away from welfare programs in order to increase investment and strengthen incentives to seek employment. The addition of 80 million people each year to an already overcrowded globe is exacerbating the problems of pollution, desertification, underemployment, epidemics, and famine. Because of their own internal problems and priorities, the industrialized countries devote insufficient resources to deal effectively with the poorer areas of the world, which, at least from the economic point of view, are becoming further marginalized. The introduction of the euro as the common currency of much of Western Europe in January 1999, while paving the way for an integrated economic powerhouse, poses economic risks because of varying levels of income and cultural and political differences among the participating nations. The terrorist attacks on the US on 11 September 2001 accentuate a further growing risk to global prosperity, illustrated, for example, by the reallocation of resources away from investment to anti-terrorist programs. The opening of war in March 2003 between a US-led coalition and Iraq added new uncertainties to global economic prospects. (For specific economic developments in each country of the world in 2002, see the individual country entries.)

GDP:
GWP (gross world product) - purchasing power parity - $49 trillion (2002 est.)

GDP – Per Capita:
purchasing power parity - $7,900 (2002 est.)

Unemployment Rate:
30% combined unemployment and underemployment in many non-industrialized countries; developed countries typically 4%-12% unemployment.

Industries:
dominated by the onrush of technology, especially in computers, robotics, telecommunications, and medicines and medical equipment; most of these advances take place in OECD nations; only a small portion of non-OECD countries have succeeded in rapidly adjusting to these technological forces; the accelerated development of new industrial (and agricultural) technology is complicating already grim environmental problems.

The World Largest Economies

Let's call this list the *World 500*. These are curently the only countries in the world with GDPs over $500 billion.

Country	Gross Domestic Product		Population		Per Capita
United States	10.45	trillion	290	million	$36,300
China	5.99	trillion	1.3	billion	$4,700
Japan	3.65	trillion	127	million	$28,700
India	2.66	trillion	1.05	billion	$2,600
Germany	2.16	trillion	82	million	$26,200
France	1.56	trillion	60	million	$26,000
United Kingdom	1.53	trillion	60	million	$25,500
Italy	1.46	trillion	58	million	$25,100
Russia	1.41	trillion	144	million	$9,700
Brazil	1.38	trillion	182	million	$7,600
Korea, South	941.50	billion	48	million	$19,600
Canada	934.10	billion	32	million	$29,300
Mexico	924.40	billion	104	million	$8,900
Spain	850.70	billion	40	million	$21,200
Indonesia	714.20	billion	234	million	$3,100
Australia	525.50	billion	19	million	$29,699

The USA is clearly the world #1 economic power. With a GDP of $10.45 trillion it's almost double its closest competitor, which is China.

In the middle of our World 500 list are the European countries – Germany, France, the United Kingdom, Italy and Spain. Individually, each country is a fraction of the economic power of the United States, but collectively they could be a powerhouse. The European countries listed above are the ones that made it onto our World 500 list.

Stop Working!

Europe, however, is in the middle of forming its own union. Remember that the United States of America is a union of states on the North American continent. The European Union (EU) is a union of states on the European continent. As of this writing, member states of this union are: Austria, Belgium, Denmark, Finland, France, Germany, Greece, Ireland, Italy, Luxemburg, the Netherlands, Portugal, Spain, Sweden and the United Kingdom. In May 2004, the following countries also joined the EU: Czech Republic, Estonia, Hungary, Latvia, Lithuania, Poland, Slovakia and Slovenia, along with Cyprus and Malta. A variety of other countries in Europe are in the process of trying to meet the qualifications of becoming an EU state.

The security threat of terrorism and the mutual benefits of this union have motivated the various states to come to a variety of agreements. One such agreement is an EU constitution that is expected to become a reality of the summer of 2004.[10]

The economic power of this new union, based on the CIA website data is as follows:

---

[10] Check out www.euabc.com for the full text of the EU Constitution and related topics

The European Union Member States

Country	Gross Domestic Product		Population		Per Capita
Germany	2.16	trillion	82	million	$26,200
France	1.56	trillion	60	million	$26,000
United Kingdom	1.53	trillion	60	million	$25,500
Italy	1.46	trillion	58	million	$25,100
Spain	850.7	billion	40	million	$21,200
The Netherlands	437.8	billion	16	million	$27,200
Poland	373.2	billion	38	million	$9,700
Belgium	299.7	billion	10	million	$29,200
Sweden	230.7	billion	8	million	$26,000
Austria	227.7	billion	8	million	$27,900
Greece	203.3	billion	10	million	$19,100
Portugal	195.2	billion	10	million	$19,400
Czech Republic	157.1	billion	10	million	$15,300
Denmark	155.3	billion	5	million	$28,900
Hungary	134	billion	10	million	$13,300
Finland	133.8	billion	5	million	$25,800
Ireland	113.7	billion	4	million	$29,300
Slovakia	67.34	billion	5	million	$12,400
Slovenia	37.06	billion	2	million	$19,200
Lithuania	30	billion	3.5	million	$8,400

Stop Working!

Luxemburg	21.94	billion	454	thousand	$48,900
Latvia	20.99	billion	2	million	$8,900
Estonia	15.52	billion	1.4	million	$11,000
Cyprus	9.4	billion	771	thousand	$15,000
Malta	6.8	billion	400	thousand	$17,200
Total	*10.43*	*trillion*	*449*	*million*	

Notice that as a union, the EU's economy of $10.43 trillion becomes #2 in the world economy. With an economy of $10.45 trillion, the United States is only slightly ahead of the EU. What does this mean for future global bargaining? What would it mean to have your products sold in the United States as well as in an economy equal to the economic size of the United States?

The World Largest Economies

The data is sorted based on population size

Country	Gross Domestic Product		Population		Per Capita
China	5.99	trillion	1.3	billion	$4,700
India	2.66	trillion	1.05	billion	$2,600
United States	10.45	trillion	290	million	$36,300
Indonesia	714.20	billion	234	million	$3,100
Brazil	1.38	trillion	182	million	$7,600
Russia	1.41	trillion	144	million	$9,700
Japan	3.65	trillion	127	million	$28,700
Mexico	924.40	billion	104	million	$8,900
Germany	2.16	trillion	82	million	$26,200
France	1.56	trillion	60	million	$26,000
United Kingdom	1.53	trillion	60	million	$25,500
Italy	1.46	trillion	58	million	$25,100
Korea, South	941.50	billion	48	million	$19,600
Spain	850.70	billion	40	million	$21,200
Canada	934.10	billion	32	million	$29,300
Australia	525.50	billion	19	million	$29,699

Notice that the countries with the greatest population on our World 500 list are China and India. These countries also have the lowest GDP - per capita. If you listen to the arguments about offshore outsourcing you'll also notice that these two countries will always be on the top of the list. Is this coincidence? Not really.

China and India have two of the largest economies in the world. It's to the advantage of the United States and other countries to have relationships with these countries to sell our products. These countries also have the lowest GDP – per capita. What this means is that the average income/production capacity for someone in India is about $2,600. It's about 10 times that much for workers in EU countries, the United States and much of the countries on our World 500 list.

To hire a qualified technical or professional person in India will probably cost you about $10,000 per year, depending on the work you would have them do. In the United States the similar type of work with similar qualifications would cost about $50,000 per year.

The fact that inexpensive, skilled workers in these countries are supported by economic treaties and agreements will allow the trend of offshore outsourcing to continue for the foreseeable future. Employers are faced with the situation of hiring an employee with a MBA, for instance, for $50,000 in the United States or hire 5 employees with the same qualification for a total of $50,000 in India. Which choice would you make?

Major corporations from all over the world are now making investments in these countries. The idea is that as these countries grow, they will need products. The products with establish placements in these countries will be naturally selected by individuals who will then be able to afford to buy them. In India and China, that's 2 billion potential customers. Wouldn't you want to have your products in a market of 2 billion potential customers?

The World Largest Economies

The data is sorted based on per capita GDP

Country	Gross Domestic Product		Population		Per Capita
United States	10.45	trillion	290	million	$36,300
Australia	525.50	billion	19	million	$29,699
Canada	934.10	billion	32	million	$29,300
Japan	3.65	trillion	127	million	$28,700
Germany	2.16	trillion	82	million	$26,200
France	1.56	trillion	60	million	$26,000
United Kingdom	1.53	trillion	60	million	$25,500
Italy	1.46	trillion	58	million	$25,100
Spain	850.70	billion	40	million	$21,200
Korea, South	941.50	billion	48	million	$19,600
Russia	1.41	trillion	144	million	$9,700
Mexico	924.40	billion	104	million	$8,900
Brazil	1.38	trillion	182	million	$7,600
China	5.99	trillion	1.3	billion	$4,700
Indonesia	714.20	billion	234	million	$3,100
India	2.66	trillion	1.05	billion	$2,600

On average, it would take 13 people in India to produce the same income as one American.

Stop Working!

The World Largest Economies

The United States of America

Country	Gross Domestic Product		Population		Per Capita
United States	10.45	trillion	290	million	$36,300

Location:
North America, bordering both the North Atlantic Ocean and the North Pacific Ocean, between Canada and Mexico

Population:
290,342,554 (July 2003 est.)

Ethnic Groups:
white 77.1%, black 12.9%, Asian 4.2%, Amerindian and Alaska native 1.5%, native Hawaiian and other Pacific islander 0.3%, other 4% (2000)

Religions:
Protestant 56%, Roman Catholic 28%, Jewish 2%, other 4%, none 10% (1989)

Languages:
English, Spanish (spoken by a sizable minority)

Economy Overview:
The US has the largest and most technologically powerful economy in the world, with a per capita GDP of $37,600. In this market-oriented economy, private individuals and business firms make most of the decisions, and the federal and state governments buy needed goods and services predominantly in the private marketplace. US business firms enjoy considerably

greater flexibility than their counterparts in Western Europe and Japan in decisions to expand capital plant, lay off surplus workers, and develop new products. At the same time, they face higher barriers to entry in their rivals' home markets than the barriers to entry of foreign firms in US markets. US firms are at or near the forefront in technological advances, especially in computers and in medical, aerospace, and military equipment, although their advantage has narrowed since the end of World War II. The onrush of technology largely explains the gradual development of a "two-tier labor market" in which those at the bottom lack the education and the professional/technical skills of those at the top and, more and more, fail to get comparable pay raises, health insurance coverage, and other benefits. Since 1975, practically all the gains in household income have gone to the top 20% of households. The years 1994-2000 witnessed solid increases in real output, low inflation rates, and a drop in unemployment to below 5%. The year 2001 saw the end of boom psychology and performance, with output increasing only 0.3% and unemployment and business failures rising substantially. The response to the terrorist attacks of 11 September 2001 showed the remarkable resilience of the economy. Moderate recovery took place in 2002, with the GDP growth rate rising to 2.45%. A major short-term problem in first half 2002 was a sharp decline in the stock market, fueled in part by the exposure of dubious accounting practices in some major corporations. The war in March/April 2003 between a US-led coalition and Iraq shifted resources to military industries and introduced uncertainties about investment and employment in other sectors of the economy. Long-term problems include inadequate investment in economic infrastructure, rapidly rising medical and pension costs of an aging population, sizable trade deficits, and stagnation of family income in the lower economic groups.

GDP:
purchasing power parity - $10.45 trillion (2002 est.)

Stop Working!

GDP- per capita:
purchasing power parity - $36,300 (2002 est.)

Unemployment Rate:
5.8% (2002)

Industries:
leading industrial power in the world, highly diversified and technologically advanced; petroleum, steel, motor vehicles, aerospace, telecommunications, chemicals, electronics, food processing, consumer goods, lumber, mining

China

Country	Gross Domestic Product		Population		Per Capita
China	5.99	trillion	1.3	billion	$4,700

Location:
Eastern Asia, bordering the East China Sea, Korea Bay, Yellow Sea, and South China Sea, between North Korea and Vietnam

Population:
1,286,975,468 (July 2003 est.)

Ethnic Groups:
Han Chinese 91.9%, Zhuang, Uygur, Hui, Yi, Tibetan, Miao, Manchu, Mongol, Buyi, Korean, and other nationalities 8.1%

Religions:
Daoist (Taoist), Buddhist, Muslim 1%-2%, Christian 3%-4% *note:* officially atheist (2002 est.)

Languages:
Standard Chinese or Mandarin (Putonghua, based on the Beijing dialect), Yue (Cantonese), Wu (Shanghaiese), Minbei (Fuzhou), Minnan (Hokkien-Taiwanese), Xiang, Gan, Hakka dialects, minority languages (see Ethnic groups entry)

Economy Overview:
In late 1978 the Chinese leadership began moving the economy from a sluggish, Soviet-style centrally planned economy to a more market-oriented system. Whereas the system operates within a political framework of strict Communist control, the economic influence of non-state organizations and individual citizens has been steadily increasing. The authorities switched to a system of household and village responsibility in agriculture in

Stop Working!

place of the old collectivization, increased the authority of local officials and plant managers in industry, permitted a wide variety of small-scale enterprises in services and light manufacturing, and opened the economy to increased foreign trade and investment. The result has been a quadrupling of GDP since 1978. In 2003, with its 1.3 billion people but a GDP of just $5,000 per capita, China stood as the second-largest economy in the world after the US (measured on a purchasing power parity basis). Agriculture and industry have posted major gains, especially in coastal areas near Hong Kong and opposite Taiwan, where foreign investment has helped spur output of both domestic and export goods. The leadership, however, often has experienced - as a result of its hybrid system - the worst results of socialism (bureaucracy and lassitude) and of capitalism (windfall gains and growing income disparities). China thus has periodically backtracked, retightening central controls at intervals. The government has struggled to (a) collect revenues due from provinces, businesses, and individuals; (b) reduce corruption and other economic crimes; and (c) keep afloat the large state-owned enterprises, many of which had been shielded from competition by subsidies and had been losing the ability to pay full wages and pensions. From 80 to 120 million surplus rural workers are adrift between the villages and the cities, many subsisting through part-time low-paying jobs. Popular resistance, changes in central policy, and loss of authority by rural cadres have weakened China's population control program, which is essential to maintaining long-term growth in living standards. Another long-term threat to growth is the deterioration in the environment, notably air pollution, soil erosion, and the steady fall of the water table especially in the north. China continues to lose arable land because of erosion and economic development. Beijing says it will intensify efforts to stimulate growth through spending on infrastructure - such as water control and power grids - and poverty relief and through rural tax reform aimed at eliminating arbitrary local levies on farmers. Accession to the World Trade Organization helps strengthen China's ability to

241

maintain strong growth rates but at the same time puts additional pressure on the hybrid system of strong political controls and growing market influences. China has benefited from a huge expansion in computer internet use. Foreign investment remains a strong element in China's remarkable economic growth.

GDP:
purchasing power parity - $5.989 trillion (2002 est.)

GDP – per capita:
purchasing power parity - $4,700 (2002 est.)

Unemployment Rate:
urban unemployment roughly 10%; substantial unemployment and underemployment in rural areas (2002 est.)

Industries:
iron and steel, coal, machine building, armaments, textiles and apparel, petroleum, cement, chemical fertilizers, footwear, toys, food processing, automobiles, consumer electronics, telecommunications

Stop Working!

Japan

Country	Gross Domestic Product		Population		Per Capita
Japan	3.65	trillion	127	million	$28,700

Location:
Eastern Asia, island chain between the North Pacific Ocean and the Sea of Japan, east of the Korean Peninsula

Population:
127,214,499 (July 2003 est.)

Ethnic Groups:
Japanese 99%, others 1% (Korean 511,262, Chinese 244,241, Brazilian 182,232, Filipino 89,851, other 237,914) (2000)

Religion:
observe both Shinto and Buddhist 84%, other 16% (including Christian 0.7%)

Languages:
Japanese

Economy Overview:
Government-industry cooperation, a strong work ethic, mastery of high technology, and a comparatively small defense allocation (1% of GDP) helped Japan advance with extraordinary rapidity to the rank of second-most-technologically-powerful economy in the world after the US and third-largest economy after the US and China. One notable characteristic of the economy is the working together of manufacturers, suppliers, and distributors in closely-knit groups called keiretsu. A second basic feature has been the guarantee of lifetime employment for a substantial portion of the urban labor force. Both features are now eroding.

Industry, the most important sector of the economy, is heavily dependent on imported raw materials and fuels. The much smaller agricultural sector is highly subsidized and protected, with crop yields among the highest in the world. Usually self-sufficient in rice, Japan must import about 50% of its requirements of other grain and fodder crops. Japan maintains one of the world's largest fishing fleets and accounts for nearly 15% of the global catch. For three decades overall real economic growth had been spectacular: a 10% average in the 1960s, a 5% average in the 1970s, and a 4% average in the 1980s. Growth slowed markedly in the 1990s, averaging just 1.7%, largely because of the aftereffects of overinvestment during the late 1980s and contractionary domestic policies intended to wring speculative excesses from the stock and real estate markets. Government efforts to revive economic growth have met with little success and were further hampered in 2000-2003 by the slowing of the US, European, and Asian economies. Japan's huge government debt, which is approaching 150% of GDP, and the ageing of the population are two major long-run problems. Robotics constitutes a key long-term economic strength with Japan possessing 410,000 of the world's 720,000 "working robots." Internal conflict over the proper way to reform the ailing banking system continues.

GDP:
purchasing power parity - $3.651 trillion (2002 est.)

GDP – per capita:
purchasing power parity - $28,700 (2002 est.)

Unemployment rate:
5.4% (2002)

Industries:

Stop Working!

among world's largest and technologically advanced producers of
motor vehicles, electronic equipment, machine tools, steel and
nonferrous metals, ships, chemicals; textiles, processed foods

India

Country	Gross Domestic Product		Population		Per Capita
India	2.66	trillion	1.05	billion	$2,600

Location:
Southern Asia, bordering the Arabian Sea and the Bay of Bengal, between Burma and Pakistan

Population:
1,049,700,118 (July 2003 est.)

Ethnic Groups:
Indo-Aryan 72%, Dravidian 25%, Mongoloid and other 3% (2000)

Religions:
Hindu 81.3%, Muslim 12%, Christian 2.3%, Sikh 1.9%, other groups including Buddhist, Jain, Parsi 2.5% (2000)

Languages:
English enjoys associate status but is the most important language for national, political, and commercial communication; Hindi is the national language and primary tongue of 30% of the people; there are 14 other official languages: Bengali, Telugu, Marathi, Tamil, Urdu, Gujarati, Malayalam, Kannada, Oriya, Punjabi, Assamese, Kashmiri, Sindhi, and Sanskrit; Hindustani is a popular variant of Hindi/Urdu spoken widely throughout northern India but is not an official language

Economy Overview:
India's economy encompasses traditional village farming, modern agriculture, handicrafts, a wide range of modern industries, and a multitude of support services. Overpopulation severely handicaps

246

the economy and about a quarter of the population is too poor to be able to afford an adequate diet. Government controls have been reduced on imports and foreign investment, and privatization of domestic output has proceeded slowly. The economy has posted an excellent average growth rate of 6% since 1990, reducing poverty by about 10 percentage points. India has large numbers of well-educated people skilled in the English language; India is a major exporter of software services and software workers; the information technology sector leads the strong growth pattern. The World Bank and others worry about the continuing public-sector budget deficit, running at approximately 10% of GDP in 1997-2002. In 2003 the state-owned Indian Bank substantially reduced non-performing loans, attracted new customers, and turned a profit. Deep-rooted problems remain, notably conflicts among political and cultural groups.

GDP:
purchasing power parity - $2.664 trillion (2002 est.)

GDP – per capita:
purchasing power parity - $2,600 (2002 est.)

Unemployment rate:
8.8% (2002)

Industries:
textiles, chemicals, food processing, steel, transportation equipment, cement, mining, petroleum, machinery, software

Germany

Country	Gross Domestic Product		Population		Per Capita
Germany	2.16	trillion	82	million	$26,200

Location:
Central Europe, bordering the Baltic Sea and the North Sea, between the Netherlands and Poland, south of Denmark

Population:
82,398,326 (July 2003 est.)

Ethnic groups:
German 91.5%, Turkish 2.4%, other 6.1% (made up largely of Serbo-Croatian, Italian, Russian, Greek, Polish, Spanish)

Religions:
Protestant 34%, Roman Catholic 34%, Muslim 3.7%, unaffiliated or other 28.3%

Languages:
German

Economy Overview:
Germany's affluent and technologically powerful economy has turned in a weak performance throughout much of the 1990s and early 2000s. The modernization and integration of the eastern German economy continues to be a costly long-term problem, with annual transfers from west to east amounting to roughly $70 billion. Germany's ageing population, combined with high unemployment, has pushed social security outlays to a level exceeding contributions from workers. Structural rigidities in the labor market - including strict regulations on laying off workers and the setting of wages on a national basis - have made

unemployment a chronic problem. Growth in 2002 and 2003 fell short of 1%. Corporate restructuring and growing capital markets are setting the foundations that could allow Germany to meet the long-term challenges of European economic integration and globalization, particularly if labor market rigidities are further addressed. In the short run, however, the fall in government revenues and the rise in expenditures have raised the deficit above the EU's 3% debt limit.

GDP:
purchasing power parity - $2.16 trillion (2002 est.)

GDP – per capita:
purchasing power parity - $26,200 (2002 est.)

Unemployment rate:
9.8% (2002 est.)

Industries:
among the world's largest and most technologically advanced producers of iron, steel, coal, cement, chemicals, machinery, vehicles, machine tools, electronics, food and beverages; shipbuilding; textiles

France

Country	Gross Domestic Product		Population		Per Capita
France	1.56	trillion	60	million	$26,000

Location:
Western Europe, bordering the Bay of Biscay and English Channel, between Belgium and Spain, southeast of the UK; bordering the Mediterranean Sea, between Italy and Spain

Population:
60,180,529 (July 2003 est.)

Ethnic groups:
Celtic and Latin with Teutonic, Slavic, North African, Indochinese, Basque minorities

Religions:
Roman Catholic 83%-88%, Protestant 2%, Jewish 1%, Muslim 5%-10%, unaffiliated 4%

Languages:
French 100%, rapidly declining regional dialects and languages (Provencal, Breton, Alsatian, Corsican, Catalan, Basque, Flemish)

Economy Overview:
France is in the midst of transition, from a well-to-do modern economy that has featured extensive government ownership and intervention to one that relies more on market mechanisms. The Socialist-led government has partially or fully privatized many large companies, banks, and insurers, but still retains controlling stakes in several leading firms, including Air France, France Telecom, Renault, and Thales, and remains dominant in some

sectors, particularly power, public transport, and defense industries. The telecommunications sector is gradually being opened to competition. France's leaders remain committed to a capitalism in which they maintain social equity by means of laws, tax policies, and social spending that reduce income disparity and the impact of free markets on public health and welfare. The current government has lowered income taxes and introduced measures to boost employment. At the end of 2002 the government was focusing on the problems of the high cost of labor and labor market inflexibility resulting from the 35-hour workweek and restrictions on lay-offs. The government was also pushing for pension reforms and simplification of administrative procedures. The tax burden remains one of the highest in Europe. The current economic slowdown and inflexible budget items have pushed the deficit above the EU's 3% debt limit. Business investment remains listless because of low rates of capital utilization, high debt, and the steep cost of capital.

GDP:
purchasing power parity - $1.558 trillion (2002 est.)

GDP – per capita:
purchasing power parity - $26,000 (2002 est.)

Unemployment rate:
9.1% (2002 est.)

Industries:
machinery, chemicals, automobiles, metallurgy, aircraft, electronics; textiles, food processing; tourism

United Kingdom

Country	Gross Domestic Product		Population		Per Capita
United Kingdom	1.53	trillion	60	million	$25,500

Location:
Western Europe, islands including the northern one-sixth of the island of Ireland between the North Atlantic Ocean and the North Sea, northwest of France

Population:
60,094,648 (July 2003 est.)

Ethnic groups:
English 81.5%, Scottish 9.6%, Irish 2.4%, Welsh 1.9%, Ulster 1.8%, West Indian, Indian, Pakistani, and other 2.8%

Religions:
Anglican and Roman Catholic 40 million, Muslim 1.5 million, Presbyterian 800,000, Methodist 760,000, Sikh 500,000, Hindu 500,000, Jewish 350,000

Languages:
English, Welsh (about 26% of the population of Wales), Scottish form of Gaelic (about 60,000 in Scotland)

Economy Overview:
The UK, a leading trading power and financial center, is one of the quartet of trillion dollar economies of Western Europe. Over the past two decades the government has greatly reduced public ownership and contained the growth of social welfare programs. Agriculture is intensive, highly mechanized, and efficient by European standards, producing about 60% of food needs with

only 1% of the labor force. The UK has large coal, natural gas, and oil reserves; primary energy production accounts for 10% of GDP, one of the highest shares of any industrial nation. Services, particularly banking, insurance, and business services, account by far for the largest proportion of GDP while industry continues to decline in importance. GDP growth slipped in 2001-03 as the global downturn, the high value of the pound, and the bursting of the "new economy" bubble hurt manufacturing and exports. Still, the economy is one of the strongest in Europe; inflation, interest rates, and unemployment remain low. The relatively good economic performance has complicated the BLAIR government's efforts to make a case for Britain to join the European Economic and Monetary Union (EMU). Critics point out, however, that the economy is doing well outside of EMU, and they point to public opinion polls that continue to show a majority of Britons opposed to the single currency. Meantime, the government has been speeding up the improvement of education, transport, and health services, at a cost in higher taxes. The war in March-April 2003 between a US-led coalition and Iraq, together with the subsequent problems of restoring the economy and the polity, involve a heavy commitment of British military forces.

GDP:
purchasing power parity - $1.528 trillion (2002 est.)

GDP – per capita:
purchasing power parity - $25,500 (2002 est.)

Unemployment rates:
5.2% (2002 est.)

Industries:
machine tools, electric power equipment, automation equipment, railroad equipment, shipbuilding, aircraft, motor vehicles and parts, electronics and communications equipment, metals,

chemicals, coal, petroleum, paper and paper products, food processing, textiles, clothing, and other consumer goods

Stop Working!

Italy

Country	Gross Domestic Product		Population		Per Capita
Italy	1.46	trillion	58	million	$25,100

Location:
Southern Europe, a peninsula extending into the central Mediterranean Sea, northeast of Tunisia

Population:
57,998,353 (July 2003 est.)

Ethnic groups:
Italian (includes small clusters of German-, French-, and Slovene-Italians in the north and Albanian-Italians and Greek-Italians in the south)

Religions:
predominately Roman Catholic with mature Protestant and Jewish communities and a growing Muslim immigrant community

Languages:
Italian (official), German (parts of Trentino-Alto Adige region are predominantly German speaking), French (small French-speaking minority in Valle d'Aosta region), Slovene (Slovene-speaking minority in the Trieste-Gorizia area)

Economy Overview:
Italy has a diversified industrial economy with roughly the same total and per capita output as France and the UK. This capitalistic economy remains divided into a developed industrial north, dominated by private companies, and a less developed, welfare-dependent agricultural south, with 20% unemployment. Most raw

255

materials needed by industry and more than 75% of energy requirements are imported. Over the past decade, Italy has pursued a tight fiscal policy in order to meet the requirements of the Economic and Monetary Unions and has benefited from lower interest and inflation rates. The current government has enacted numerous short-term reforms aimed at improving competitiveness and long-term growth. Italy has moved slowly, however, on implementing needed structural reforms, such as lightening the high tax burden and overhauling Italy's rigid labor market and over-generous pension system, because of the current economic slowdown and opposition from labor unions.

GDP:
purchasing power parity - $1.455 trillion (2002 est.)

GDP – per capita:
purchasing power parity - $25,100 (2002 est.)

Unemployment rate:
9.1% (2002 est.)

Industries:
tourism, machinery, iron and steel, chemicals, food processing, textiles, motor vehicles, clothing, footwear, ceramics

Russia

Country	Gross Domestic Product		Population		Per Capita
Russia	1.41	trillion	144	million	$9,700

Location:
Northern Asia (that part west of the Urals is included with Europe), bordering the Arctic Ocean, between Europe and the North Pacific Ocean

Population:
144,526,278 (July 2003 est.)

Ethnic groups:
Russian 81.5%, Tatar 3.8%, Ukrainian 3%, Chuvash 1.2%, Bashkir 0.9%, Belarusian 0.8%, Moldavian 0.7%, other 8.1% (1989)

Religions:
Russian Orthodox, Muslim, other

Languages:
Russian, other

Economy Overview:
A decade after the implosion of the Soviet Union in December 1991, Russia is still struggling to establish a modern market economy and achieve strong economic growth. In contrast to its trading partners in Central Europe - which were able within 3 to 5 years to overcome the initial production declines that accompanied the launch of market reforms - Russia saw its economy contract for five years, as the executive and legislature dithered over the implementation of many of the basic foundations of a market economy. Russia achieved a slight

recovery in 1997, but the government's stubborn budget deficits and the country's poor business climate made it vulnerable when the global financial crisis swept through in 1998. The crisis culminated in the August depreciation of the ruble, a debt default by the government, and a sharp deterioration in living standards for most of the population. The economy subsequently has rebounded, growing by an average of more than 6% annually in 1999-2002 on the back of higher oil prices and the 60% depreciation of the ruble in 1998. These GDP numbers, along with a renewed government effort to advance lagging structural reforms, have raised business and investor confidence over Russia's prospects in its second decade of transition. Yet serious problems persist. Oil, natural gas, metals, and timber account for more than 80% of exports, leaving the country vulnerable to swings in world prices. Russia's industrial base is increasingly dilapidated and must be replaced or modernized if the country is to maintain vigorous economic growth. Other problems include a weak banking system, a poor business climate that discourages both domestic and foreign investors, corruption, local and regional government intervention in the courts, and widespread lack of trust in institutions. In 2003 President PUTIN further tightened his control over the "oligarchs," especially in the realm of political expression.

GDP:
purchasing power parity - $1.409 trillion (2002 est.)

GDP – per capita:
purchasing power parity - $9,700 (2002 est.)

Unemployment rate:
7.9% plus considerable underemployment (2002)

Industries:
complete range of mining and extractive industries producing coal, oil, gas, chemicals, and metals; all forms of machine

Stop Working!

building from rolling mills to high-performance aircraft and space vehicles; shipbuilding; road and rail transportation equipment; communications equipment; agricultural machinery, tractors, and construction equipment; electric power generating and transmitting equipment; medical and scientific instruments; consumer durables, textiles, foodstuffs, handicrafts

Brazil

Country	Gross Domestic Product		Population		Per Capita
Brazil	1.38	trillion	182	million	$7,600

Location:
Eastern South America, bordering the Atlantic Ocean

Population:
182,032,604

Ethnic groups:
white (includes Portuguese, German, Italian, Spanish, Polish) 55%, mixed white and black 38%, black 6%, other (includes Japanese, Arab, Amerindian) 1%

Religions:
Roman Catholic (nominal) 80%

Languages:
Portuguese (official), Spanish, English, French

Economy Overview:
Possessing large and well-developed agricultural, mining, manufacturing, and service sectors, Brazil's economy outweighs that of all other South American countries and is expanding its presence in world markets. The maintenance of large current account deficits via capital account surpluses became problematic as investors became more risk averse to emerging markets as a consequence of the Asian financial crisis in 1997 and the Russian bond default in August 1998. After crafting a fiscal adjustment program and pledging progress on structural reform, Brazil received a $41.5 billion IMF-led international support program in November 1998. In January 1999, the Brazilian Central Bank

announced that the real would no longer be pegged to the US dollar. The consequent devaluation helped moderate the downturn in economic growth in 1999, and the country posted moderate GDP growth in 2000. Economic growth slowed considerably in 2001-03 - to less than 2% - because of a slowdown in major markets and the hiking of interest rates by the Central Bank to combat inflationary pressures. New president DA SILVA, who took office 1 January 2003, has given priority to reforming the complex tax code, trimming the overblown civil service pension system, and continuing the fight against inflation.

GDP:
purchasing power parity - $1.376 trillion (2002 est.)

GDP – per capita:
purchasing power parity - $7,600 (2002 est.)

Unemployment rate:
6.4% (2001 est.)

Industries:
textiles, shoes, chemicals, cement, lumber, iron ore, tin, steel, aircraft, motor vehicles and parts, other machinery and equipment

Korea, South

Country	Gross Domestic Product		Population		Per Capita
Korea, South	941.50	billion	48	million	$19,600

Location:
Eastern Asia, southern half of the Korean Peninsula bordering the Sea of Japan and the Yellow Sea

Population:
48,289,037 (July 2003 est.)

Ethnic groups:
homogeneous (except for about 20,000 Chinese)

Religions:
Christian 49%, Buddhist 47%, Confucianist 3%, Shamanist, Chondogyo (Religion of the Heavenly Way), and other 1%

Languages:
Korean, English widely taught in junior high and high school

Economy Overview:
As one of the Four Tigers of East Asia, South Korea has achieved an incredible record of growth and integration into the high-tech modern world economy. Three decades ago GDP per capita was comparable with levels in the poorer countries of Africa and Asia. Today its GDP per capita is 18 times North Korea's and equal to the lesser economies of the European Union. This success through the late 1980s was achieved by a system of close government/business ties, including directed credit, import restrictions, sponsorship of specific industries, and a strong labor

Stop Working!

effort. The government promoted the import of raw materials and technology at the expense of consumer goods and encouraged savings and investment over consumption. The Asian financial crisis of 1997-99 exposed longstanding weaknesses in South Korea's development model, including high debt/equity ratios, massive foreign borrowing, and an undisciplined financial sector. Growth plunged to a negative 6.6% in 1998, then strongly recovered to 10.8% in 1999 and 9.2% in 2000. Growth fell back to 3.3% in 2001 because of the slowing global economy, falling exports, and the perception that much-needed corporate and financial reforms had stalled. Led by consumer spending and exports, growth in 2002 was an impressive 6.2%, despite anemic global growth, followed by moderate 2.8% growth in 2003. In 2003 the six-day work week was reduced to five days.

GDP:
purchasing power parity - $941.5 billion (2002 est.)

GDP – per capita:
purchasing power parity - $19,600 (2002 est.)

Unemployment rate:
3.1% (2002 est.)

Industries:
electronics, automobile production, chemicals, shipbuilding, steel, textiles, clothing, footwear, food processing

Canada

Country	Gross Domestic Product		Population		Per Capita
Canada	934.10	billion	32	million	$29,300

Location:
Northern North America, bordering the North Atlantic Ocean on the east, North Pacific Ocean on the west, and the Arctic Ocean on the north, north of the conterminous US

Population:
32,207,113 (July 2003 est.)

Ethnic groups:
British Isles origin 28%, French origin 23%, other European 15%, Amerindian 2%, other, mostly Asian, African, Arab 6%, mixed background 26%

Religions:
Roman Catholic 46%, Protestant 36%, other 18%
note: based on the 1991 census

Languages:
English 59.3% (official), French 23.2% (official), other 17.5%

Economy Overview:
As an affluent, high-tech industrial society, Canada today closely resembles the US in its market-oriented economic system, pattern of production, and high living standards. Since World War II, the impressive growth of the manufacturing, mining, and service sectors has transformed the nation from a largely rural economy into one primarily industrial and urban. The 1989 US-Canada Free Trade Agreement (FTA) and the 1994 North American Free Trade Agreement (NAFTA) (which includes Mexico) touched off

Stop Working!

a dramatic increase in trade and economic integration with the US. As a result of the close cross-border relationship, the economic sluggishness in the United States in 2001-02 had a negative impact on the Canadian economy. Real growth averaged nearly 3% during 1993-2000, but declined in 2001, with moderate recovery in 2002. Unemployment is up, with contraction in the manufacturing and natural resource sectors. Nevertheless, given its great natural resources, skilled labor force, and modern capital plant Canada enjoys solid economic prospects. Two shadows loom, the first being the continuing constitutional impasse between English- and French-speaking areas, which has been raising the specter of a split in the federation. Another long-term concern is the flow south to the US of professionals lured by higher pay, lower taxes, and the immense high-tech infrastructure. A key strength in the economy is the substantial trade surplus.

GDP:
purchasing power parity - $934.1 billion (2002 est.)

GDP – per capita:
purchasing power parity - $29,300 (2002 est.)

Unemployment rate:
7.6% (2002 est.)

Industries:
transportation equipment, chemicals, processed and unprocessed minerals, food products; wood and paper products; fish products, petroleum and natural gas

Mexico

Country	Gross Domestic Product		Population		Per Capita
Mexico	924.40	billion	104	million	$8,900

Location:
Middle America, bordering the Caribbean Sea and the Gulf of Mexico, between Belize and the US and bordering the North Pacific Ocean, between Guatemala and the US

Population:
104,907,991 (July 2003 est.)

Ethnic groups:
mestizo (Amerindian-Spanish) 60%, Amerindian or predominantly Amerindian 30%, white 9%, other 1%

Religions:
nominally Roman Catholic 89%, Protestant 6%, other 5%

Languages:
Spanish, various Mayan, Nahuatl, and other regional indigenous languages

Economy Overview:
Mexico has a free market economy with a mixture of modern and outmoded industry and agriculture, increasingly dominated by the private sector. Recent administrations have expanded competition in seaports, railroads, telecommunications, electricity, natural gas distribution, and airports. Income distribution remains highly unequal. Trade with the US and Canada has tripled since the implementation of NAFTA in 1994. Following 6.9% growth in 2000, real GDP fell 0.3% in 2001, recovering to only a plus 1% in 2002, with the US slowdown the principal cause. Mexico

Stop Working!

implemented free trade agreements with Guatemala, Honduras, El Salvador, and the European Free Trade Area in 2001, putting more than 90% of trade under free trade agreements. Foreign direct investment reached $25 billion in 2001, of which $12.5 billion came from the purchase of Mexico's second-largest bank, Banamex, by Citigroup.

GDP:
purchasing power parity - $924.4 billion (2002 est.)

GDP – per capita:
purchasing power parity - $8,900 (2002 est.)

Unemployment rate:
urban - 3% plus considerable underemployment (2002)

Industries:
food and beverages, tobacco, chemicals, iron and steel, petroleum, mining, textiles, clothing, motor vehicles, consumer durables, tourism

Spain

Country	Gross Domestic Product		Population		Per Capita
Spain	850.70	billion	40	million	$21,200

Location:
Southwestern Europe, bordering the Bay of Biscay,
Mediterranean Sea, North Atlantic Ocean, and Pyrenees
Mountains, southwest of France

Population:
40,217,413 (July 2003 est.)

Ethnic groups:
composite of Mediterranean and Nordic types

Religions:
Roman Catholic 94%, other 6%

Languages:
Castilian Spanish 74%, Catalan 17%, Galician 7%, Basque 2%
note: Castilian is the official language nationwide; the other
languages are official regionally

Economy Overview:
Spain's mixed capitalist economy supports a GDP that on a per
capita basis is 80% that of the four leading West European
economies. Its center-right government successfully worked to
gain admission to the first group of countries launching the
European single currency (the euro) on 1 January 1999. The
AZNAR administration has continued to advocate liberalization,
privatization, and deregulation of the economy and has
introduced some tax reforms to that end. Unemployment has been

Stop Working!

steadily falling under the AZNAR administration but remains high at 11.7%. The government intends to make further progress in changing labor laws and reforming pension schemes, which are key to the sustainability of both Spain's internal economic advances and its competitiveness in a single currency area. A general strike in mid-2002 reduced cooperation between labor and government. Growth of 2.4% in 2003 was satisfactory given the background of a faltering European economy. Adjusting to the monetary and other economic policies of an integrated Europe - and reducing unemployment - will pose challenges to Spain over the next few years.

GDP:
purchasing power parity - $850.7 billion (2002 est.)

GDP – per capita:
purchasing power parity - $21,200 (2002 est.)

Unemployment rate:
11.3% (2002 est.)

Industries:
textiles and apparel (including footwear), food and beverages, metals and metal manufactures, chemicals, shipbuilding, automobiles, machine tools, tourism

Indonesia

Country	Gross Domestic Product		Population		Per Capita
Indonesia	714.20	billion	234	million	$3,100

Location:
Southeastern Asia, archipelago between the Indian Ocean and the Pacific Ocean

Population:
234,893,453 (July 2003 est.)

Ethnic groups:
Javanese 45%, Sundanese 14%, Madurese 7.5%, coastal Malays 7.5%, other 26%

Religions:
Muslim 88%, Protestant 5%, Roman Catholic 3%, Hindu 2%, Buddhist 1%, other 1% (1998)

Languages:
Bahasa Indonesia (official, modified form of Malay), English, Dutch, local dialects, the most widely spoken of which is Javanese

Economy Overview:
Indonesia, a vast polyglot nation, faces severe economic development problems stemming from secessionist movements and the low level of security in the regions; the lack of reliable legal recourse in contract disputes; corruption; weaknesses in the banking system; and strained relations with the IMF. Investor confidence will remain low and few new jobs will be created under these circumstances. In November 2001, Indonesia agreed

Stop Working!

with the IMF on a series of economic reforms in 2002, thus enabling further IMF disbursements. Negotiations with the IMF and bilateral donors continued in 2002. Keys to future growth remain internal reform, the build-up of the confidence of international donors and investors, and a strong comeback in the global economy.

GDP:
purchasing power parity - $714.2 billion (2002 est.)

GDP – per capita:
purchasing power parity - $3,100 (2002 est.)

Unemployment rate:
10.6% (2002 est.)

Industries:
petroleum and natural gas; textiles, apparel, and footwear; mining, cement, chemical fertilizers, plywood; rubber; food; tourism

271

Australia

Country	Gross Domestic Product	Population	Per Capita
Australia	525.50 billion	19 million	$29,699

Location:
Oceania, continent between the Indian Ocean and the South
Pacific Ocean

Population:
19,731,984 (July 2003 est.)

Ethnic groups:
Caucasian 92%, Asian 7%, aboriginal and other 1%

Religions:
Anglican 26.1%, Roman Catholic 26%, other Christian 24.3%,
non-Christian 11%, other 12.6%

Languages:
English, native languages

Economy Overview:
Australia has a prosperous Western-style capitalist economy,
with a per capita GDP on par with the four dominant West
European economies. Rising output in the domestic economy has
been offsetting the global slump, and business and consumer
confidence remains robust. Australia's emphasis on reforms is
another key factor behind the economy's strength. The stagnant
economic conditions in major export partners and the impact of
the worst drought in 100 years cast a shadow over prospects for
2003.

Stop Working!

GDP:
purchasing power parity - $525.5 billion (2002 est.)

GDP – per capita:
purchasing power parity - $26,900 (2002 est.)

Unemployment rate:
6.3% (2002)

Industries:
mining, industrial and transportation equipment, food processing, chemicals, steel

Rohan Hall

Favorite Downloads

I think we live in an amazing time. I call it amazing because we can now sit at home and purchase a book online to learn a wealth of information from people we have never met, and probably will never meet. I like a scene in the movie *The Matrix*, when the main character is plugged into a knowledge base and downloads the information he needs directly to his brain. I believe our ability to learn from people with decades of experience by simply buying a book, listening to a tape, watching a TV show, seeing a movie, or gathering information from the internet is a privilege that no other generation before us have had. *Stop Working!* is an expression of 20 years of my personal business experience and I hope you had a successful download of the information presented.

Below, are some of my favorite downloads that I've found fascinating, interesting, educational and even life changing over the years. I currently have no affiliation with any of these authors but I find their work to be pretty cool!

Anthony Robbins
The first time I listened to Tony Robbins tapes I wanted to go out and change *my* world ... which I did. I am still a big fan of his work.

Dale Carnegie – How to Win Friends and Influence People
I didn't believe this book when I read it first. I thought it was too simple so I had to test the different points mentioned myself. I was amazed and am still influenced by that book today. I use the techniques daily even though I read the book about 20 years ago.

Robert Kiyosaki – Rich Dad Series
When I read *Rich Dad, Poor Dad and The Cashflow Quadrant*, I remember thinking – this guy has really got it! It's required reading for anyone who wants to stop working.

Rohan Hall

About the Author

Mr. Hall has spent the last 20 years helping companies develop global business and technology strategies. Some companies he has provided services to include: Hewlett Packard, PeopleSoft, Corning, Honda, Avery Dennison, Lockheed, Boeing, The American Red Cross, Sierra Pacific Power Company, and Robert Half International. He has provided services for these companies primarily in the United States but also in Europe and Asia.

He is the owner and CEO of vConcepts, Inc., a professional services company that focuses on the integration of technology and business processes for large organizations through Enterprise Resource Planning (ERP).

He is also the owner and CEO of Eye Contact Media, Inc., the publisher of this book.